D1064956

Teaching Through Projects

Creating Effective Learning Environments

Heidi Goodrich

Thomas Hatch

Gwynne Wiatrowski

Chris Unger

Project Zero, Harvard Graduate School of Education

Innovative Learning Publications

Addison-Wesley Publishing Company

Menlo Park, California ■ Reading, Massachusetts ■ New York

Don Mills, Ontario ■ Wokingham, England ■ Amsterdam ■ Bonn

Paris ■ Milan ■ Madrid ■ Sydney ■ Singapore ■ Tokyo ■ Seoul

Taipei ■ Mexico City ■ San Juan

This book is published by Innovative Learning Publications™, an imprint of the Alternative Publishing Group of Addison-Wesley Publishing Company.

Senior Editor: Lois Fowkes

Design Manager: Jeff Kelly

Production/Manufacturing Director: Janet Yearian

Production/Manufacturing Coordinator: Michael Nealy

Cover and text design: Paula Shuhert

Composition: Andrea Reider

Illustration: Margaret Sanfilippo
Walt Shelly

ISBN 0-201-49507-4

  2 3 4 5 6 7 8 9 10-ML-99 98 97 96

"Having the kids step back and look at what they've done and know that they worked hard to do something well is very rewarding. To watch these children grow socially, emotionally, academically, it's wonderful. You find kids who I guess over the years were sort of lost, and I feel like they've been found. They found themselves, which I think is the most important thing that can happen for a child— for them to recognize that they do mean something, they are an important part of this world, and they have something to contribute."

—Traci
Teacher in the Mather Afterschool Program

C O N T E N T S

A C K N O W L E D G M E N T S

The Mather Afterschool research project was supported in part by Pew Charitable Trusts, the John D. and Catherine T. MacArthur Foundation, and the Spencer Foundation. The program itself was supported in part by Freedom House through a grant from New England Telephone. The contents of this guidebook are solely the responsibility of the authors.

The principal investigators for this project are Williamill Damon of Brown University and Howard Gardner and David Perkins of Harvard Graduate School of Education.

The authors would like to thank the other members of our research team: Celeste Bowman-Brown, Deb Brazil, Deb Bullock, Allan Collins, Joyce Conkling, Roger Dempsey, Carol Gignoux, Dominique Gilmer, Sabine Pierre Jules, Michael K. Marshall, Uyen Chi Nguyen, Majid Rashaad, Thu-Hang Tran, and Traci Turner.

A portion of the proceeds from the sale of this book will go toward the continuation of project-based education and the afterschool program at the Mather School.

INTRODUCTION

Several years ago, an interviewer asked a sixth grader why she went to school. The student looked confused and responded, "But I thought you knew!"

All too often, students don't know why they are in school or why what they are doing in the classroom is important. Instead, students are often left with the impression that they are doing math, writing essays, or studying a foreign language simply because they have to, because the teacher or the school requires it. As a result, students often have little motivation to become personally engaged in classroom activities, and they may never discover the uses and values of their skills and knowledge outside of school.

This problem is not unique to students. Teachers too are frequently required to use materials they do not endorse or to teach topics that don't particularly appeal to them. Instead of responding to the specific needs and interests of their students, district policies and national testing practices often force them to move on to the next chapter of a textbook or the next topic of a mandated curriculum. Consequently, teachers have little incentive to engage their students in activities that reflect their concerns or that are directly relevant to their school and community.

The goal of this guidebook is to help teachers and students carry out projects that foster learning and that mean something to them.

What Are Projects?

Projects are long-term, problem-focused, and meaningful activities that bring together ideas and principles from a number of subject areas or disciplines.

Teaching through projects is not a new idea. Project-based approaches to education have been tried before, but they have often been thought of as too difficult to implement in most schools and as ineffective for teaching basic skills. Over the years, however, a number of educators have endorsed project-based learning, and individual teachers and schools have used projects successfully. Our own experience has shown that, when carefully thought out, projects are manageable and educationally effective.

Projects are especially good teaching tools for the following reasons:

Projects motivate students to learn about and use a wide variety of literacy and thinking skills.

For example, publishing a newspaper gives students opportunities to plan, write, reflect on, and revise articles, and provides a way in which the students can share their work with others.

Projects encourage students to become self-directed thinkers and learners.

Unlike many classroom activities, projects enable students to take the lead in their own learning. In the process, they develop the skills and dispositions they need to initiate, pursue, and complete work without explicit directions from or close supervision by their teachers.

Projects give teachers opportunities to use innovative teaching techniques.

Because projects encourage students to be self-directed, teachers are able to act as coaches and can vary their level of support to suit the needs of individual students. Projects also provide students with incentives to work together and share their expertise. In addition, projects yield numerous occasions for students to demonstrate their progress and to get direct feedback from teachers, peers, and outside experts.

**Projects can be used both in classrooms
and in programs outside of school.**

By providing opportunities for students to develop literacy and
thinking skills, projects can satisfy many of the traditional
demands of the regular school day while increasing students'
interest and motivation. At the same time, because projects are
not viewed as "schoolwork," students are willing to become
involved in them even in settings that are usually reserved for
purely recreational pursuits, such as afterschool programs.

A Brief History of Our Project

The educational promise of projects has been demonstrated
inside and outside of school and with students of all ages and
backgrounds. The examples you will encounter in this book
are drawn from an afterschool program developed through a
collaboration between university researchers and teachers and
the principal at a local elementary school.

We had three basic goals for the program. First of all, we wanted
to help students who were having difficulty in school become
self-directed thinkers and learners. Second, we wanted to support teachers' attempts to try out innovative teaching strategies
and curricula that may have seemed too unproven or unfamiliar
for immediate use in the classroom. Third, we hoped that the
program would encourage and be a model for effective learning
environments both inside and outside of school.

The program's home was the Mather School in Dorchester,
Massachusetts. Located in the Boston area, the school's
student body was 48% African American, 33% Asian, 14%
white, 5% Hispanic, and 1% Native American in 1993. Seventy-
six percent of the 640 students received free or reduced-price
meals, more than half lived with a single parent, and over one
third came from homes where English was not spoken.

Each school year, the program served forty-five students from
the third, fourth, and fifth grades. Although the program was

open to all, our selection process focused on students who were thought to be at risk of social or academic failure. Students met four days a week in mixed-grade groups with a total of six teachers from the school. They worked on a wide variety of projects, ranging from publishing a newspaper to cooking to organizing a clothing drive for the homeless.

More information about our program can be found in Appendix A. We would like to emphasize, however, that the usefulness of a project-based approach to teaching is not limited to our particular location, students, or afterschool context. Projects have worked and will continue to work at all grade levels, with all types of students, and during the regular school day as well as after school.

About This Guide

This guidebook is designed to give teachers and other educators the tools they need to develop successful projects. It is not a collection of activities that can be implemented directly. Rather, it is a set of principles, strategies, and techniques to help teachers design projects that draw on their own and their students' interests and concerns.

The guidebook can be used in a number of ways. It is intended for those who are interested in using projects in their classrooms or programs, but it also includes ideas and strategies for improving the organization, operation, and effectiveness of any educational setting. For those who are interested in developing their own projects, Chapter 1 reviews the essential characteristics of a successful project. Chapter 2 overviews a number of classroom-tested projects that you may want to try or at least borrow ideas from. Since involving students in projects is not enough to ensure they will learn, Chapter 3 discusses several teaching strategies that can increase the educational effectiveness of projects. Because thoughtful planning is critical to the success of a project, Chapter 4 offers a guide to the project design process. And finally, since carrying out a project for the first time can be difficult, Chapter 5 discusses the challenges of "doing projects" and offers some advice on how to handle them.

Defining Successful Projects

" You should see children being very self-directed. You should see the teacher . . . acting as coach. You should see . . . a lot of peer collaboration going on. You should see maybe a lot of materials and different information available for the students. I think it should be a very relaxed atmosphere where the room is basically being run by the students. I think that would be an ideal project. Where an observer sees a lot less lecturing and a lot more doing. "

—Traci

A Portrait of a Successful Project

The Better World Environmental Project engages students in generating and carrying out solutions to local environmental problems. Here, to give you the flavor of a successful project, is a peek into the classroom during the early days.

Students enter the classroom and immediately head for the windowsills, where their zinnia seedlings are soaking up the sun. After carefully tending to their plants, the students collect in a group around their teacher, who tells them what they need to do to prepare for their chosen project, a school-wide recycling drive. The list is long and diverse: someone has to write a letter to the principal, asking him to include an announcement about the recycling drive in the next parent memo; someone has to make flyers advertising the recycling drive and put one in each teacher's mailbox; someone has to find a recycling business in the phone book and call to arrange for a pickup of the recyclables; several people have to make posters and hang them in strategic places in the school; and others have to round up and label collection boxes and distribute them in the hallways.

The students volunteer for the tasks that interest them and get to work, either alone or with a friend. The teacher writes the information necessary for the letter, flyers, and posters on the board and ensures that writers and poster-makers know they need to include this information in their various announcements. She directs them to the materials and turns her attention to Shameaka, who volunteered to make the phone call. A fifth grader, Shameaka has questions about what to say and what questions to ask. Together they rehearse the call and decide what information she should be sure to get. Shameaka writes all this down and promises to take notes about the call.

As the girl sets off for the office to use the phone, two fourth-grade boys announce that they are finished with their posters. The teacher has a look but doesn't yet offer her own comments. Instead, she asks them what they think of each poster, probing for specific strengths and possible improvements. They are by now used to being asked to think critically about their work, so they explain what they like about their posters and make one or two good suggestions for revision. The teacher then points out a spelling error they overlooked, and the boys get back to work.

It isn't long before both boys are finished and satisfied with their posters. The teacher, who is now helping a fourth-grade girl with her flyer, agrees that the posters are ready to hang and sends the boys out into the school with a roll of masking tape. When they return, they start the process again—making posters, critiquing their own and each other's work, revising their posters, and hanging them up in the hall.

Everyone is so engaged and self-directed that the teacher is able to pause and survey the room for several minutes. She sees small groups of students busily working on a variety of tasks that they chose themselves. She muses about the fact that many of these students resist these same tasks—writing, for example—in more traditional contexts but not in this project. Her reverie is interrupted by Shameaka, who is back from the office with information about the recycling business.

Five Characteristics of Successful Projects

Our early experiments with projects, including the Better World Environmental Project, varied in terms of how actively involved students and teachers became in them, how easy they were to implement, and the degree to which they promoted our learning goals for the children. Our observations and discussions, as well as comments from our students, revealed that the more successful projects tended to share certain features. Successful projects

- involve topics and activities that are of **genuine interest** to both the teacher and the students

- provide a **natural context for learning**

- have clear **goals and steps**

- are **flexible** in terms of which tasks are taken on by students and how they are approached

- permit and encourage a high degree of **self-direction** on the part of the students

Projects Are of Genuine Interest

> When we first started [using reflection worksheets], I didn't like it. Sometimes it was like pulling teeth with these kids. But once the project became something that was interesting to them, they came up with a lot of good answers, they really did reflect on what they did, and I found that it was working.
>
> —*Sabine*

A genuine project is *motivating* and *authentic* to the teacher as well as to the students. Without these elements, neither students nor teachers are likely to have the sustained attention needed to accomplish the goals of the project and learn from what they are doing. Motivation, of course, comes from choosing topics, tasks, and goals that everyone truly cares about. The Field Trip Project has students choose, plan, and organize their own trips. It is motivating because the students love going on field trips of their own choice. It is authentic because, after doing a substantial amount of planning, writing, and organizing, they actually go on the trip. The project is motivating to their teacher because she is able to combine fun with teaching literacy and thinking skills to her students.

Authenticity, on the other hand, comes from involving students in "real" work toward "real" products.

Having grown up in this era of heightened awareness of environmental problems, students come to the Better World Environmental Project with a fair amount of knowledge and passion about environmental issues. Their teacher makes the most of their motivation by giving them the opportunity to engage in authentic projects, such as a recycling drive, which help alleviate one or more of the problems students are concerned about.

Projects Provide a Natural Context for Learning

> [M]ost of the projects that I did were projects that were meaningful to the kids and to me. The project has to be something that will incorporate academics like writing and reading, but you make it more fun for them so they do it and they're not saying, 'Oh, I have to sit down and write.' It's something that they want to do anyway.
>
> —Dominique

Students who generally refuse to write or do math problems when a task too closely resembles "schoolwork" do not hesitate when these same tasks appear in the context of a genuine project. Given the option, nonwriters often do write, and mathphobes do calculate. This is because these tasks fit naturally within the goals of the projects, rather than being force-fit in order to fulfill externally imposed curriculum requirements.

The Field Trip Project is a good example of a natural fit between learning goals and project goals. This teacher has her students figure out how much money they need for a trip and then write a clear and convincing proposal to the people in charge of cash disbursements. In this way, mathematics, writing, and reasoning skills become natural parts of arranging a trip.

This is not to say, however, that projects provide an excuse to overlook important learning goals. As the example of nonwriters and mathphobes shows, we have found projects to be well suited to the promotion of valuable skills, *provided the skills are necessary steps in reaching the genuine goals of the project.* We stress this point because it is both important to recognize and tricky to implement. The tendency among educators is to begin by identifying learning goals—literacy, cooperative learning, or whatever—then to attempt to build projects around them. Although such an approach can occasionally work, too many projects designed in this way flop.

An example of the need for learning goals to fit naturally into the context of a project can be found in our early efforts to include "reflection" in our projects. In an attempt to help students critically review their work and the work of others, we had them fill out "reflection sheets" at the end of a project. The reflection sheets asked them to write down what was good about the work done during the project, what was not so good about it, and how it could be improved.

At best, we got cursory answers to each question, not the thoughtful reflection we'd hoped for. This led us to rethink the role of reflection in the project. We quickly realized that it is natural for students to reflect before creating their final products, when they still have time to revise their work. We also acknowledged that it makes sense to give and receive feedback verbally as well as in writing. We then organized "feedback sessions" in which students shared their work with the group and received verbal feedback about what was good and not so good about it, as well as how it could be improved. The students responded enthusiastically and became quite adept at giving, receiving, and using constructive criticism.

Projects Have Clear Goals and Steps

> "You have to have steps . . . goals and objectives to follow so you can know why you're doing it, what you're doing it for, and the purpose of it. . . . That's the first thing . . . what you want to do, how you're going to do it, how you're going to set it up."
>
> —*Carol*

The kind of sustained work required by relatively long-term endeavors like projects requires that students understand what they are working toward and what they will need to do to get there. Because project work is unfamiliar to many students, the goals of a project and the steps involved in reaching them need to be made explicit from the start.

There are at least two ways to make a project's goals clear to your students. One is to have the students decide the goals of the project themselves. Another is to begin by telling students what the goals are and then to discuss the goals to make sure they understand what you mean.

Having clear goals or products is not enough, however. It is also important to clarify the often complex steps involved in achieving these goals. Again, there are several ways to accomplish this. One approach is to use a problem-solving framework or strategy like the one on pages 10–11. Such a framework allows students to anticipate the steps they will take in the project they are currently engaged in and to know what to expect when they move on to other projects that use the same framework. Although this particular framework may not be appropriate for every project, the general notion of a "process backbone,"—or consistent steps across projects—makes it easier for students to succeed.

In the Better World Environmental Project, the teacher informs the students of the general goal of "saving the earth" and then helps them generate ideas and choose from among the many earth-friendly project possibilities.

The Field Trip Project has an advantage in terms of clear goals and processes because field trips are common activities and so are familiar to students. However, the project also requires students to create brochures advertising their trip and to present the work done in the project at an exhibition. The students are informed of these goals when they begin to work on the project.

Both projects use a problem-solving framework to make the processes involved in reaching the goals of the projects clear. The framework has eight steps: (1) get background information, (2) decide on your purpose, (3) brainstorm ideas, (4) carefully select the best idea, 5) make a first draft, (6) get feedback, (7) make revisions, and (8) prepare the final draft.

For example, in the Better World Environmental Project, the teacher presents information about environmental problems (Step 1 in the framework), then asks students what should be done about them (Step 2), and has students generate a list of things they can do to help solve those problems (Step 3). The group settles on one or more ideas by discussing the pros and cons of each (Step 4). Then everyone gets to work on plans, letters, posters, or whatever is necessary to reach their goal (Step 5). When their work is ready, students get feedback (Step 6) and revise their work accordingly (Step 7).

SMART THINKING

1 Get Background Information

2 Decide on Your Purpose

Smart Rules to Follow:

- List many goals.
- Mark the most important and practical goals.
- Choose the two or three most important and practical goals.

3 Brainstorm

Smart Rules to Follow:

- Think of lots of ideas.
- Think of imaginative ideas.
- No dissing any ideas.

4 Carefully Select

Smart Rules to Follow:

- Ask: What are the two or three most promising ideas?
- Ask: What are the good and bad points of each idea?
- Ask: Pick the best idea or put the best parts of each idea together.

5 Make First Version

(of plan, product, or writing)

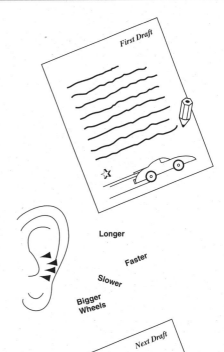

First Draft

6 Get Feedback

Smart Rules to Follow:

- Ask: What's good?
- Ask: What could be better?
- Ask: How can we do that?

Longer

Faster

Slower

Bigger Wheels

7 Make Revisions

Smart Rules to Follow:

- Think about which improvements are the most important.
- Choose the ones you want to make.
- Make the improvements.

Next Draft

8 Give Final Presentation/Exhibition

Projects Are Flexible

> *Gwynne:* What's important to remember when doing projects?
>
> *Celeste:* To know that, doing a project, nothing is written in stone. . . . You can change ideas. You can add to [or] subtract from your original concept as you see the progress of the project.

At first glance, this fourth characteristic of a successful project may appear to conflict with the third characteristic, *clear goals and processes.* After all, how is it possible to allow for flexibility in terms of which tasks are taken on and how they are approached if one has established clear products and processes? The key to the conflict is *options.* Although it is important to make the goals of a project clear, it is possible and even critical for a teacher to be flexible about where the project will go and how students will get it there. This means having a few different ideas about possible activities and responding to student interests by asking for their ideas and giving them choices about what they do. This kind of flexibility allows students to work according to their own styles and intelligences, and often results in a greater sense of ownership.

Students in the Better World Environmental Project decide for themselves which environmental problems they will tackle. This often means that two or three different goals are being pursued at once, allowing the teacher to take advantage of each group's particular interests and contributing to the genuineness of the project. The teacher is prepared to add activities and roles as necessary, ensuring that children can contribute to the project in their own ways—by writing, providing leadership, drawing, making telephone calls, or whatever task best matches project needs to student strengths and interests.

The Field Trip Project provides flexibility by allowing each subgroup of three or four students to decide on the destination for their trip. Although the entire group eventually goes on each trip, this approach allows the students in each small group to have a real voice in the decision about where to go. This project also provides for flexibility in terms of tasks and approaches by allowing the students to decide who will make phone calls, who will do the math needed to calculate the costs of the trip, who will write a proposal for money to fund the trip, and so on.

Projects Encourage Self-Direction

> [The project approach] allows the students to be in charge of their own learning. It allows them to create, to come up with a plan, to see the plan through to the finish, to learn from their mistakes and their successes, and to reflect on it, figure out what they can do better next time.
>
> —*Carol*

We place *self-direction* last on our list of characteristics of a good project because it is both the consequence of creating a project that contains the first four characteristics and an important characteristic in its own right. That is, a project encourages and requires student self-direction when it is genuine to the teacher and students, has clear goals and steps, is flexible in terms of tasks and approaches to them, and has a natural fit between its learning goals and the goals of the project.

Taken together, the first four characteristics make it possible for students to do a remarkable amount of independent work—independent of the teacher, that is. Perhaps the most visible difference between the "traditional" classroom and the project-based classroom is the role of the teacher. Teachers in project-based classrooms rarely stand at the front of the room and lead a group of students through a lesson plan. Rather, they can most often be found acting as coaches or facilitators to small groups of students, answering their questions, giving them feedback when they want it, or finding a role for the student who is disruptive or not participating.

The teacher-as-coach role requires both the fulfillment of the first four characteristics of a good project—genuineness, a natural context for learning, clear goals and steps, and flexibility—as well as the commitment of the teacher to experiment with a new role in the classroom. The Better World Environmental Project described on pages 3 and 4 illustrates this relationship between student self-direction and coaching.

2

Sample Projects

This chapter gives an overview of many classroom-tested projects that served specific goals. In order to help students become self-directed thinkers and learners, we designed our projects to foster three kinds of skills: writing, reflection, and problem-solving. Meeting these learning goals meant engaging students in a variety of authentic writing tasks, supporting them as they reviewed the quality of their own and each other's work, and teaching them to take a problem-solving approach to a wide variety of tasks. As a result, the examples presented in this guidebook often involve activities linked to one or more of these skills. Nonetheless, these projects could easily be adapted to focus on a wide variety of academic, social, and personal goals (although we recommend focusing on only a few at a time!).

Each of the projects outlined below took our mixed groups of third-, fourth-, and fifth-grade students about sixteen one-and-one-quarter-hour sessions to finish. You will notice that we list the steps of each project without giving more specific time estimates for implementation. We took this approach because projects are flexible and can vary widely in how long a particular step takes, depending on the teacher, the students, and the context.

The way a project plays out in the classroom can also vary a lot. In fact, there are as many ways to implement a project as there are teachers. Space limitations as well as respect for your creativity as a teacher keep us from listing every activity appropriate for every project. These project outlines, therefore, are designed to give you a general feel for how a project might play out as well as give enough detail to help you develop a clear mental model of what happens and when and how it happens. Accordingly, the first project that follows is written up in detail to get you started, with key terms in italics. The remaining projects are offered in outline form.

The Newspaper Project in Detail

Overview

Writing stories, drawing advertisements and cartoons, editing, doing layout, and copying and distributing the newspaper are the responsibilities students assume as publishers of their own newspaper.

Goal

To publish a student newspaper.

Learning Goals for Students

To learn how to write and revise a news story, an editorial, or a review.
To learn how to give and receive feedback.
To learn how to lay out a newspaper.
To learn a careful and systematic approach to doing good work.

The Steps

STEP 1

Introducing the project

The teacher, Traci, begins by going over the daily *routines* students can expect within the project. There are numerous ways to introduce students to routines.

OPTIONS

- This teacher hands out copies of an agenda for the day (see page 19) and tells students that each day will begin with ten minutes of journal writing, then a large-group meeting during which they will review the agenda for that day, and then small-group or individual work on articles, etc.
- Another teacher might post the routines on the wall or board.

- Another might physically walk students through the routine, quickly moving from the journal writing area to the group meeting area to the individual work stations, and so on.

Agenda for Tuesday, May 10

Journals

Group meeting

Write/work on news stories

Optional (when you have finished your news story):

    Design an advertisement

    Create a cartoon

    Read quietly

    Do homework

Traci goes on to explain the *layout of the classroom* in terms of the functions of each space, then begins to talk about the project. She tells the groups that they are going to create their own newspaper. She has students look at actual newspapers. The group discusses why people read newspapers and the different kinds of information found in a newspaper.

STEP

2

Determining criteria

Traci then helps her students decide on the criteria for a good newspaper. She does so by showing students copies of a newspaper created by a previous group and asking them to list the "good things" and "not-so-good things" about it. When they have voiced all their opinions about the sample paper, Traci asks them to make a list of criteria for their own newspaper.

Students draw on their earlier lists to generate the criteria for a newspaper they can be proud of (see below). Traci posts the new list for easy reference later. Other approaches to determining criteria include:

- Having students look at real newspapers and list their characteristics.

- Having students compare "good" and "poorly done" newspapers (professional or student-generated) and discuss what makes one good and the other poor.

- Having small groups of students focus on particular sections of a newspaper and determine the criteria for that section only.

- Having students interview a newspaper editor about what he or she demands of a paper.

Criteria for a Good Newspaper

The articles, reviews, and so on must

- tell who, what, where, when
- have correct spelling
- make sense
- be brief but informative—no unnecessary repetition
- be interesting

The newspaper itself must

- be neatly put together (good layout)
- be organized like a real newspaper

Planning the newspaper

Referring to professional and student newspapers, Traci's class creates a list of the different features of a newspaper—headlines, comics, sports, photos, ads, and so on. They then decide on the purpose of their newspaper and which features to include by considering their audience and asking questions like: Who will get copies of the newspaper? What will they want to know? What will make them want to read the paper?

Making goals and steps clear

Traci helps students identify the responsibilities involved in creating the paper and assigns *roles* accordingly. Then she

The Newspaper Checklist

_____ Brainstorm a list of topics

_____ Pick your favorite topic

_____ Make a first draft (of an article, review, ad, cartoon, etc.)

_____ Check your work: Does it meet our criteria?

_____ Get feedback

_____ Revise

_____ Have a teacher conference

_____ Make a final draft

_____ Layout

_____ Copying

_____ Distribution

_____ Reflection: How did it turn out? How did it go?

gives each student a checklist to keep in their folders. The checklist outlines the process students will go through to get an article, ad, or anything at all published in the paper. She briefly goes over the checklist. Using a previous student's work as an example, she retells the story of how that student's article went through a series of information collection, writing, feedback, revising, and so on.

To encourage students to transfer their knowledge of this process to other contexts, Traci points out other times and places when a similar process would be useful: When writing a book report, doing a painting, performing a dance or song, and so on.

Writing

Traci tells students that she is going to show them how to write a first draft of an article. She *models* the writing process by writing a news story on a large sheet of paper. Thinking out loud, she demonstrates how she chooses a topic and answers the questions: who, what, where, when, and how. Afterward, students begin work on their own articles, ads, and cartoons.

O P T I O N S

- For an editorial or a review, a teacher might do a similar activity, answering the same questions but also including opinions. This teacher would emphasize the need for evidence or support for opinions.

- A local reporter might be asked to talk to the class about the process she goes through when writing and producing an article.

Giving and receiving feedback

Collecting the students in a large group, Traci informs them that there is a particular way she wants them to give and receive *feedback* about the quality of their work. She writes the rules of constructive feedback on a chart and posts it on the wall: (1) First talk about the strengths of the work in terms of the criteria the class generated, then (2) Express your concerns about it in terms of the criteria, then (3) Suggest ways to make improvements. Traci *coaches* her students in giving feedback on one student's work, then asks students to get into groups of two or three and give each other verbal feedback.

Teaching Through Projects

- Students could give each other feedback in writing. A feedback form like the one on page 24 could help to keep the criticism constructive.

STEP 7 — Revising

Students continue working in pairs or individually, as they wish, to edit their work. Students also meet with Traci for short conferences before writing a final draft.

STEP 8 — Laying out, copying, and distributing the newspaper

Students cut and paste final drafts of news articles, ads, comics, photos, headlines, and so on to create a page or section. They photocopy and collate the final draft of the layout and distribute it to the students and teachers in the school.

O P T I O N

- Ideally, students would do all the cutting, pasting and layout on the computer. Classes without computers or the appropriate software can do all of this work by hand.

STEP 9 — Reflecting on the project

The teacher leads the group in a discussion of what they liked about their newspaper and what they would change if they were to do it again. She asks them to think about the same questions in terms of how well they approached their work: What parts of the process did they do well? What didn't go so well? What should they do differently next time?

O P T I O N S

- Journals are excellent reflection tools. A teacher might ask students to reflect on their work and their approach to work in a journal entry.

- Another teacher might have had students list criteria for how they approach their work (the process) as well as the results of their work (the product—an article or whatever they produced) early in the project. Students could then assess for themselves the way they carried out their work.

Feedback Form

Who did the work?

_____

Who gave feedback?

_____

Signature _____ Date _____

This is what I think is good about your work (refer to the criteria).

This is what I think could be better about your work (refer to the criteria).

Here are a few suggestions for how you might make your work better.

⚜ Making It Work in the Classroom

Much of the student work in this project is independent or takes place in small groups; therefore a consistent classroom *routine* is essential for a productive work environment. Daily planning meetings in which the teacher introduces new activities, reviews the day's agenda (which lists the required and optional tasks), and assigns *roles* and responsibilities can provide the necessary structure to the students' independent work.

The Business Project

⚜ Overview

In this project, students make, market, and sell holiday-related crafts such as paper flowers for Valentine's Day or felt banners with "pro-mom" messages for Mother's Day. Students decide on a craft, estimate the amount they'll need to make, secure a loan, advertise the sale with posters, make the crafts, sell them to students and teachers, and write proposals for how the proceeds should be spent.

⚜ Goal

To make money!

⚜ Learning Goals for Students

To learn how to estimate sales and profits.
To learn how to write a persuasive proposal.
To learn how to work together cooperatively.
To learn the rudiments of starting a business: securing
    a loan, selling a product, repaying the loan, and making a
    profit.
To learn how to handle money.

░▓░▓░▓ The Steps

STEP 1

Introducing the project

The teacher introduces the project and informs students of the steps they will be going through, including brainstorming a list of products to sell, advertising their product, estimating the amount they will need to make, getting a loan, making the products, selling them, and writing proposals.

STEP 2

Brainstorming

The teacher leads the group in a discussion of which holidays are approaching and what products they might sell. They then give pros and cons for each item on the list (cost of materials and complexity of design are often major considerations) and choose a product.

STEP 3

Making estimates

Students use information about the population of the school and past Business Project sales to estimate how much product they will need. Next, they estimate the cost of materials and the price of their product.

STEP 4

Securing a loan

A small group of students writes a letter to their teacher (or another adult in charge of cash disbursements), outlining their plan and its potential costs and profits. After receiving feedback from other students, the group submits the letter and receives either the loan or a request for more information from the "bank."

STEP 5

Advertising

While one group writes for a loan, the rest of the students work on advertising by making and hanging posters, asking the principal to announce the sale on the public address system, and so on.

STEP 6

Making the product

Students work furiously to meet their quota, making flowers, pom-poms, banners, or whatever product they have chosen for several days at a time.

Teaching Through Projects

STEP 7

Selling the product

Students sell their product, usually during lunch time in the cafeteria. Afterward, the proceeds are counted and the "bank" is repaid.

STEP 8

Writing proposals

Students write letters in which they propose and support an idea for what to do with the proceeds from their sale. Before they begin, their teacher has them decide on the criteria that will be used to identify the best proposal.

STEP 9

Feedback and criteria-setting

The students share their proposals and receive feedback.

STEP 10

Revising

Students revise their proposals to better fit the criteria.

STEP 11

Choosing a proposal

The teacher or the group decides which proposal is the best, and the money is spent accordingly. If the decision is to throw a party or go on a field trip, the students handle all of the planning and implementation.

Making It Work in the Classroom

One key to the success of this project is allowing several things to go on at once, rather than having each student work on the same task at the same time. Guiding and supporting a class full of students engaged in a variety of tasks means paying special attention to classroom management. This teacher began each day with an "open circle" meeting, during which students gave updates on what they had accomplished so far, listed the things that still needed to be done, and volunteered to do certain tasks. The necessary materials were readily accessible, so students could get right to work once they knew what they were doing.

The Games Project

※ Overview

This project has students invent new board games using recycled materials. Students are taught to think like inventors and to establish criteria for their games through exploration, play, and discussion. An initial sketch of a game and a draft of directions are prepared by each student, who then receives feedback from his or her classmates before producing a final version.

※ Goal

To create new board games that are fun and relatively easy to play, either by adapting other games or coming up with new ideas.

※ Learning Goals for Students

To understand the fundamentals of games—what makes them fun and challenging time after time.
To learn how to write and follow directions.
To learn how to give and receive constructive feedback.
To learn to think and work inventively by brainstorming, sketching ideas, getting feedback, and revising.

The Steps

Introducing the project

The teacher presents the project goal and activities. Using a model game, she explains the steps for inventing a new game: establishing criteria or standards for games, making a first draft, receiving feedback, reflecting on the feedback, and creating a final draft.

Establishing criteria

In order to help the group create a list of criteria for a game, the teacher provides students with opportunities to play different board games and reflect on the qualities that make a game "good." Then they brainstorm a list of features for their criteria. For example, if "fun to play" is one criterion, they may say that using a spinner is one way to help a game meet that criterion.

O P T I O N

- The group can poll other children, asking them to list the criteria for a good game and to identify how a game meets their criteria.

Creating a first draft

Each student brainstorms ideas for a game, chooses the idea which he or she thinks will work best given the list of criteria, and then sketches a picture of what the game might look like. A draft of directions for playing the game is also prepared.

Giving and receiving feedback

Using the model game from the introduction, the teacher shows students how to best give feedback: to talk about the ways the game does and does not meet the criteria and to give suggestions for improvement. Students then give and receive feedback in large or small groups.

Making a final draft

Once students have finished giving and receiving feedback, they gather the necessary materials and complete a final, polished version of their game.

Celebrating with a game day

The students organize a Game Day, during which they play each other's games.

✡ Making It Work in the Classroom

Like many others, this project requires a classroom structure that can guide students through the steps of the project while at the same time encouraging them to work independently. Strategies that promote this kind of self-directed learning environment include: a consistent classroom routine; regular large-group meetings; and a checklist or poster outlining the steps students need to complete in the project. In addition, short teacher conferences can help both students and the teacher check the progress of student work, as well as ensure that the group's chosen criteria are being addressed.

The Cooking Project

✡ Overview

In this project, students make delicious treats. In order to make these snacks, students need to: select a recipe and estimate how much it will cost to prepare; write a proposal to convince the teacher and their classmates to select their recipe; and decide which recipe to make first by helping to identify the best proposal.

✡ Goal

To make delicious treats!

✡ Learning Goals for Students

To learn how to estimate prices and create a budget.
To learn how to write a persuasive proposal.
To learn how to work together cooperatively.
To learn how to cook, including following written directions and using fractions to measure ingredients.

The Steps

STEP 1

Introducing the projects

The teacher introduces the project and informs students of the steps they will be going through, including choosing recipes, writing proposals, and cooking together.

STEP 2

Estimating prices

The teacher leads students in a game of "The Price Is Right." In this game the students get a list of snack items and are asked to estimate how much each item costs. Then the teacher models how she estimates prices. The students compare and contrast estimates and real prices (found in grocery–store circulars), then play the "The Price Is Right" again.

STEP 3

Choosing recipes

Each student receives a collection of simple recipes (see Appendix B) and chooses a recipe that she or he would like to make.

STEP 4

Introducing proposal writing

The teacher introduces the proposal-making process. In this introduction, she

- Explains what the proposal should contain, including a description of what the students want to make, at least three reasons why they think the class should make it, and a budget.

- Provides an example of a good proposal.

- Models how to write a proposal.

- Provides a "proposal-writing checklist" (see page 32) to guide students in checking their work.

Proposal-Writing Checklist

Is your proposal:

____ Well organized?

____ Grammatically correct?

____ Spelled correctly?

____ Neat?

Does your proposal:

____ State your name and the date?

____ Tell what you want to make?

____ List the ingredients?

____ Estimate the cost of the ingredients?

____ Explain how you figured the prices?

____ Give three good reasons for making the recipe?

STEP 5

Writing proposals

The students work on their proposals in small groups while the teacher acts as coach. See the example of a student's work on page 33.

Dear Mrs Gilmer,
My name is Ebony Maxwell I am 9 years old In the 4th grade group 3. I am going to tell you a little about my recipe here are the Ingredients. 4 oranges 4 apples 4 bunches of seedless grapes 4 bananas. Now I am going to Estimate. I think that the 4 oranges will cost $1.99. I also think that the 4 oranges will also cost $1.99. Following I think 4 bunches of seedless grapes will cost $200 or $300. Finaly I think the 4 bananas will cost $1.99. My Opinion of why we should cook this recipe because the recipe is healthy the recipe won't make your teeth fall out. I also think the recipe is go because there's alot of good fruits I am going to tell you what my recipe is a fruit salad.

STEP 6

Giving and receiving feedback

The students share their proposals and get feedback from each other and the teacher.

STEP 7

Revising

Students revise their proposals.

STEP 8

Selecting the best proposal

The first time around, the teacher selects the best proposal and explains how she made her decision. After that, the group decides which proposal is the best.

STEP 9

Cooking

Working in small groups, students prepare the recipe from the best proposal.

STEP 10

Doing the project again

The teacher introduces another collection of recipes and the recipe selection and the cooking process are repeated. This time around, the teacher has students help her identify all the proposals that meet the criteria laid out in the proposal-writing checklist, then has students vote on which of the recipes from that list to make.

OPTION

- Taking a trip to the grocery store to check the prices of real items and buy ingredients; playing "The Price Is Right" at the end of the project to see if students' estimating skills have improved; organizing a game of "The Price Is Right" for other students and parents at an open house; providing refreshments at an open house or parents' night; having students make cookbooks; and having the students invent their own recipes.

Making It Work in the Classroom

Like many others, this project relies on a consistent classroom routine. Each day begins with journal writing. The journals are used to give students time to write freely about whatever they choose and to give their teacher time to organize materials. After about five minutes of writing, they get into groups. The teacher states the goals of the day, gives directions, and answers questions. The students then engage in a self-directed activity such as writing or cooking while the teacher acts a coach, helping those who need it. Those who finish early can read a book, do a puzzle, work on homework, assist another group, or write in their journals. Near the end of the day, all student work is collected, the room is cleaned up, and everyone gets a snack.

The Cultural Celebrations Project

Overview

Students explore their cultural heritage through the creation of a scrapbook that includes a description of the student and his or her family, a family portrait, a family tree, a map of the country or countries the student's family is from, and additional information such as favorite family recipes. In addition, students learn about one particular culture represented in their school community (for example, African American, Cape Verdean, or Vietnamese).

⍟ Goals

To understand and appreciate the customs and traditions of the child's own and other cultures.

To create a cultural scrapbook representing the child's cultural background.

⍟ Learning Goals for Students

To learn more about personal family history and cultural heritage.

To understand and appreciate the customs and traditions of a racial or ethnic group from the school community.

To identify multiple sources of information (for example, parents, books, maps, and so forth) for the scrapbooks.

To improve writing skills.

To practice verbal presentation skills.

To learn to work in small groups or individually in a self-directed, independent manner.

The Steps

Introducing the project

The goals of the project are explained and illustrated by sharing cultural scrapbooks prepared by the teacher or previous students. Students introduce themselves and tell about their racial or ethnic identity. The group shares ideas about the meaning of the word *culture*. The teacher articulates her expectations for classroom behavior and outlines daily routines such as journal writing and group meeting time.

Writing a family description

In preparation for their family portrait collage, students are asked to write a physical description of their family members. Using her own scrapbook as an example, the teacher explains the importance of thinking about physical characteristics when choosing materials to make the portrait. The teacher points out how varied skin tones and hair color among members of her family influenced decisions about the materials she used.

STEP 3

Giving and receiving feedback

Students review their written descriptions with the teacher or a peer.

STEP 4

Making a family portrait

Students use collage materials to construct a portrait of their family members.

STEP 5

Exploring cultural backgrounds

Students gather information from family members, maps, and books about their own cultural heritage and complete related pages in their scrapbook—including a family tree, a map of their or their ancestors' country of origin, a family recipe, and so on. Students share this information about themselves and their families during the large-group sharing time at the beginning of the day. Occasionally, visitors from other countries not represented in the student body come to talk about their cultures.

STEP 6

Taking a closer look at one culture

Students alternate work on their own scrapbooks with activities designed to teach them about the cultural traditions of a specific racial or ethnic group represented in the school community. Activities can relate to a traditional celebration of the culture being studied. For example, our students learned about the principles of Kwanzaa and made crafts to give as gifts in their celebration of Kwanzaa at the end of the fall term.

STEP 7

Hosting a cultural celebration

Students celebrate in the manner of the culture they have been learning about. They also display or present their cultural scrapbooks during a school-wide exhibition.

⚉ Making It Work in the Classroom

The teacher who designed this project relies heavily on establishing consistent classroom routines in the first few meetings and on using checklists or daily agendas to structure classroom activities. Students enter the classroom and write in their journals at the beginning of each day. Then the teacher passes around an agenda for the day, which the group reviews before beginning a sharing period or individual work. In addition, the teacher gives all students a checklist for keeping track of the different pages to be included in their scrapbooks.

The Jewelry Project

⚉ Overview

Students design and create jewelry with a variety of materials including beads, buttons, macaroni, string, leather, and clay. Students also write step-by-step directions for reproducing their jewelry designs. The directions are published in a craft book, which is distributed to other students.

⚉ Goal

To design jewelry, and to write and publish directions for making each piece.

⚉ Learning Goals for Students

To learn to think creatively and to produce appealing artwork.
To learn how to write clear directions and requests for
    materials.
To learn how to plan carefully.
To learn to give and receive feedback.

✷≋✷≋✷≋ The Steps

STEP **1**	### Introducing the project

The teacher begins by explaining the project goals and reviewing a project checklist, which clearly outlines each step in the process of planning, making, and writing about jewelry. Students then explore and experiment with the craft materials they will be using.

STEP **2**	### Planning

The teacher models how to sketch a jewelry design and writes a list of materials for her design. Students sketch their design ideas, select one, and write a list of materials.

STEP **3**	### Giving and receiving feedback

Students share their sketches and lists of materials with each other and/or the teacher, and get feedback.

STEP **4**	### Revising

If necessary, students revise their design ideas and lists of materials.

STEP **5**	### Creating the design

Students collect their materials and make their jewelry.

STEP **6**	### Writing directions

The teacher models how to write directions. Each student then writes detailed, step-by-step directions for creating her or his piece.

STEP **7**	### Testing the directions

Students test each other's directions by trying to recreate a design simply by following the directions. If there are problems making the jewelry, the directions are checked for lack of clarity and, if necessary, are revised. The teacher may also check the directions for clarity, grammar, and spelling.

STEP 8

Writing a final draft

Students may use a computer or carefully rewrite the directions by hand for inclusion in the craft book.

STEP 9

Creating a book

Each child creates a page with a drawing or photo of her or his jewelry design, a list of materials, and step-by-step directions for inclusion in the jewelry-making book. The book is distributed to other students, teachers, and parents.

✗ Making It Work in the Classroom

As with most projects, a consistent daily routine aids in the creation of a self-directed classroom environment. Each meeting of the Jewelry Project begins with a large-group meeting during which a checklist is distributed. Students are asked to complete the checklist as they progress through the steps of the project.

The Bookmaking Project

✗ Overview

Students write, illustrate, and put together books about themselves or some other topic of interest. They may create more than one book, and they may work cooperatively to create books with other children.

✗ Goal

To write, illustrate, design, and assemble a book.

✗ Learning Goals for Students

To learn and practice a step-by-step approach to writing.
To learn about the different parts of a book.
To learn to work cooperatively.

The Steps

STEP 1

Introducing the project

The teacher explains the project's goal and how students will accomplish this goal. She shares examples of student-made books or a model she created herself so that the goal will be clear to the students.

STEP 2

Identifying a purpose and audience

Individually or in a large group, students think about why they want to write a book (to tell a story, to report an event, and so on) and who will read it.

STEP 3

Establishing criteria

Students read books by other children and review different kinds of books (fairy tales, mysteries, science fiction, biographies, and so on). The group brainstorms a list of qualities that make a book "good" and choose a set of criteria for their own books. The final list is posted in the classroom or copied for each student to refer to throughout the writing process.

STEP 4

Writing a first draft

Students begin the writing process by brainstorming a list of things they would like to write about. Then they outline the important information in their stories (for example, who, what, where, and when) and collect any additional information they might need. When they are ready, they compose a first draft.

STEP 5

Getting feedback and revising

The teacher reminds students to refer to the list of criteria established in Step 3 while giving or getting feedback. Students review their own writing before asking peers or a teacher to read it. The peers or teacher tell the student what they like and suggest changes or improvements. Students revise their writing according to the feedback.

STEP 6   Illustrations and cover artwork

Students work on drawings or other types of illustrations for their books. Each student designs a cover for his or her book.

O P T I O N

- Students may work on illustrations throughout the project by alternating writing days with art-production days.

STEP 7   Publishing a final draft

Students assemble the writing, illustrations, and cover to create the final draft of their book. Each book is cataloged and displayed in the library.

⚸ Making It Work in the Classroom

This teacher uses a writing checklist that outlines the steps of the writing process in order to provide structure and to allow students to work at their own pace. She reviews and models each step the first time students try it. She also holds brief teacher-student conferences during which they check the progress of the student's work. Classroom arrangement also plays a central role in this project. Groups of tables or desks provide areas for small-group work or space for students to work independently without being isolated. However, a few places for solitary student work are important for those children who want or need to be alone to concentrate. The room also has a separate reading space and library area. This space not only allows children to read quietly—an alternative activity closely related to the project's goals—it also provides a public place where students can display their work and read other students' books.

The Better World Environmental Project

Overview

Today's students know a lot about global environmental problems, but little about local problems and what they can do about them. This project has students tackle real environmental problems as well as share their concerns and knowledge about the environment with others in the school.

Goal

To design and implement real solutions to real environmental problems.

Learning Goals for Students

To understand humankind's relationship to the earth.
To learn to use a problem-solving strategy.
To learn to give and receive feedback.
To learn that they can make a difference and help solve environmental problems.

The Steps

STEP 1

Getting background information

The teacher begins by having students collect information from various sources, including:

- The video *The Rotten Truth*, produced by Children's Television Workshop, 1990.
- Guest speakers, such as the owner of a local recycling center, or people from environmental groups like The Audubon Society or the Massachusetts Public Interest Research Group (MassPIRG). Students brainstorm a list of questions for each speaker before he or she arrives.

- Hands-on activities such as making recycled paper, investigating wasteful practices by comparing the weight of a small cereal box to the cereal it contains, or learning to sort trash according to what is and is not recyclable.

- Books and magazines.

STEP 2

Brainstorming ideas

After collecting information, students brainstorm ideas for possible solutions to the problems they learned about and for an exhibit at the end of the term.

- Ideas for solutions have included: planting trees or flowers; making birdhouses out of milk cartons; writing letters to politicians; searching the school trash for recyclable or redeemable material; having a recycling drive or starting a recycling program in the school; going on a litter drive; cleaning up the wooded lot next to the school; making stuffed animals from old clothes; and replacing the wasteful utensil packets used in the cafeteria.

- Ideas for the exhibit have included: a play or skit; videotaped public service announcements; written articles to submit to the Newspaper Project; slides or a videotaped show of what they did to save the earth; pamphlets or books; trivia quizzes; posters; raps; bookmarks with slogans; and toys, games, art, and other products made out of reused materials.

STEP 3

Choosing and planning

Once they've come up with a good list of options, students decide on what they are interested in working on and make a plan for carrying it out. Planning involves listing the tasks that need to be done and deciding who will do what. For example, organizing a recycling drive requires that the following tasks are taken care of by one or more people:

- Making and hanging posters that announce the recycling drive.

- Writing, copying, and distributing flyers that give information about the recycling drive.

- Collecting, labeling, and distributing collection crates and boxes.

- Sorting the things that people bring in.

- Taking redeemable cans and bottles to the local recycling center or telephoning recycling centers to arrange for a pickup.

STEP 4
Giving and receiving feedback

If students are doing work that will be seen by others, such as posters, flyers, or rap performances, they get feedback from each other about what is good and not so good about it and how it can be improved.

O P T I O N

- Students are asked to evaluate their own work in terms of what is good and not so good and what could be improved.

STEP 5
Revising

After getting feedback, students take time to revise their work.

STEP 6
Making the final products

Students' final products range from a recycling drive (after which they need to decide what to do with the money earned from redeemables) to performances and displays for the exhibit.

✵ Making It Work in the Classroom

This project often ends up having several things going on at once, such as making phone calls, hanging posters, and writing a flyer. In order to orchestrate all these activities, the teacher begins each day with a brief group meeting in which students are told what needs to be done and asked to volunteer for tasks. Once the tasks are settled, the students are self-directed, leaving the teacher free to act as a coach, moving from group to group and helping as necessary.

The Better World Social Project

⌗ Overview

Social problems like homelessness, drug abuse, and violence are important issues for many students. This project has students design and implement solutions to these problems as well as share their concerns and actions with others in the school.

⌗ Goal

To do something to help the homeless, curb drug abuse, or end violence, or create a performance with a prosocial message.

⌗ Learning Goals for Students

To understand the complex network of causes of social problems.
To learn to use a problem-solving strategy.
To learn to give and receive feedback.
To learn that they can help alleviate local social problems.

⌗≋⌗≋⌗≋ The Steps

Getting background information

Although students know a lot about various social problems, they tend not to think in terms of what they themselves can do about them. Therefore, the project begins with a little information, focusing on the causes of social problems and how they can be prevented, solved, or alleviated.

OPTIONS

■ Invite guest speakers, such as someone from a local homeless shelter. They can answer students' questions about homelessness and have them make sandwiches for distribution to the homeless.

- Hold class discussions about personal experiences with homelessness, drug abuse, or violence and what can be done about these issues.

- Read books and newspapers like the homeless newspaper, *Spare Change* (published by HEP/SPARE CHANGE, 1151 Massachusetts Avenue, Cambridge, MA 02138).

STEP 2

Brainstorming ideas

While they collect information and afterward, students brainstorm ideas for solving or alleviating the problems they've been hearing about, as well as for sharing their ideas at an exhibit.

- Ideas for solutions have included organizing a clothing drive; making crafts or food to sell and donating the proceeds to the homeless; and writing to government officials urging them to do something.

- Ideas for the exhibit have included making books, writing articles for the newspaper; and performing raps and dances.

STEP 3

Choosing and planning

Students choose the project they are interested in working on and get to work, usually in groups or pairs.

STEP 4

Giving and receiving feedback

Written work, performances, and ideas are regularly shared with the whole group during feedback sessions. The group comments on what is good about the work, what is not so good, and how it can be improved.

STEP 5

Revising

After getting feedback, students take time to polish their work.

STEP 6

Making the final products

Students' products have included books, articles, bulletin-board displays, skits, raps and dances, and a clothing drive for the homeless.

Making It Work in the Classroom

In order for students to be engaged, it is important that they are allowed to choose which projects they will work on. Given a choice of several projects, it is the rare student who can't find anything to interest him or her. As with other projects, orchestrating several different projects at once requires that the teacher act as a facilitator, setting each student up with a task, then moving from group to group and helping when necessary.

The Etching Arts Project

Overview

In this project, students design and create a gold-foil etching and display their work along with a written explanation of what the etching symbolizes. Students begin by etching and writing about Egyptian drawings. (Another option is for the project to focus on another style of art, or no particular style at all.) Then they design, create, write about, and display their own original etchings.

Goals

To create etchings on gold foil.
To provide a written explanation of what students' etchings symbolize to them.

Learning Goals for Students

To learn how to draft, sketch, and create an etching.
To learn how to draft and craft a detailed written explanation.
To learn how to give and receive feedback.
To learn how art can act as a form of communication.

◈≋◈≋◈≋ The Steps

STEP 1

Introducing the project

The teacher introduces the project and informs students of the steps they will be going through, including discussing the nature of Egyptian art, exploring the process of creating sketches, and providing a detailed explanation of one's artwork.

STEP 2

Sketching

Students select and sketch two pieces of Egyptian art.

STEP 3

Giving and receiving feedback

Students get feedback from each other about their initial sketches. The teacher coaches them to talk about which sketches they like and why, and to make suggestions for improvement.

STEP 4

Sketching

Based on feedback and their own personal interest, students select one sketch and improve it for the final etching.

STEP 5

Etching

Pressing hard with a pencil or pen, students trace their final drawing with gold-tone aluminum foil underneath. They turn the foil over to see the imprint.

STEP 6

Listing messages and symbols

Students list different messages and themes they see in their artwork.

STEP 7

Drafting an explanation

Working from their lists, students draft explanations of their artwork. Their teacher reminds them to answer these questions: What is it called? What does it symbolize? What does it mean to them? Detail of explanation is stressed.

STEP 8

Giving and receiving feedback

Students share their works of art and explanations with other students and their teacher. About their explanations, they ask: What do you like about it? What concerns do you have? Do you have any recommendations for improving it?

STEP 9

Rewriting

Students rewrite their explanations based on the feedback.

STEP 10

Displaying the work

Students attach their etchings and explanations to poster-boards and display them in the classroom.

STEP 11

Brainstorming

Students brainstorm a list of drawings they would like to create to symbolize a variety of themes and issues from their lives.

STEP 12

Making initial drafts

Students draft several pieces of personal artwork.

STEP 13

Giving and receiving feedback

Students get feedback regarding their initial sketches.

STEP 14

Making a final sketch

Students select the one sketch they would like to develop into an etching and etch it on gold foil.

STEP 15

Having an exhibition

Students repeat Steps 3 through 8 above and display their final pieces of artwork at an exhibition for the school and community.

Making It Work in the Classroom

In the beginning of the project, the teacher who designed it showed students several examples of art, so that they could discuss symbols and representations in artwork, and so that students would not get hung up on not having anything to draw. When they became familiar with the process, he encouraged them to create their own drawings. He also stressed the importance of student self-assessment. When students ran up to him to ask for approval—"Is this good?"—he would reply, "What do you think?" The result was that students became critical evaluators of their own artwork.

The Bulletin Board Project

Overview

Students design bulletin boards for their school in this project. The bulletin-board design process involves determining what makes a good board, giving and receiving feedback on first drafts, and displaying final bulletin boards.

Goal

To make bulletin boards for display in the school.

Learning Goals for Students

To learn how to design visual displays with a message.
To learn how to work together to develop the best ideas.
To learn how to use the Smart Thinking problem-solving strategy (explained on pages 10–11).

The Steps

STEP 1

Introducing the project

The teacher introduces the project by asking students to tell him what a bulletin board is. He asks, "What are they for? Why do people have them? How are they used?" Together he and his class develop a list of the purposes of bulletin boards.

STEP 2

Gathering information

Students learn about the features of bulletin boards by looking at examples around the school and neighborhood and in books and magazines.

STEP 3

Modeling

The teacher creates a quick first draft of a bulletin board as students watch and make suggestions. As he works, he models the thought processes involved in deciding on a topic, choosing materials, and experimenting with color and layout.

STEP 4

Giving and receiving feedback

The teacher asks the group to give him feedback on his bulletin board (verbally or in writing). He asks, "What worked about our first attempt? What didn't work? What could we improve?"

STEP 5

Determining criteria

The teacher asks students to list the features of a good bulletin board by looking at his draft and thinking about what they thought worked and didn't work. He asks, "What are the elements of a good bulletin board?"

STEP 6

Choosing themes

As a large group, students brainstorm possible bulletin-board themes (see example on page 53). To encourage creativity, the teacher writes down all their ideas without criticism or praise. The students then select several themes from the list, organize themselves in small groups, and discuss the message they want their board to send.

Bulletin Board Theme Brainstorm

Sports

Books

Trees

Drugs

Freedom

Education

Grass

Easter

Violence

Strangers

Art

Flowers

Ocean

Clothing

STEP

7

Making a first draft

Students design a small-scale draft of their bulletin boards in their small groups. The teacher coaches them to sketch the layout of their boards and include a write-up of the intended message. He also asks students to write a list of the materials they will need to actually create the boards.

STEP 8

Giving and receiving feedback

Each group presents their draft and gets feedback from the large group. The teacher encourages the group to refer to their list of the elements of a good bulletin board when giving feedback.

STEP 9

Revising

Students revise their drafts, incorporating the feedback into their revisions.

STEP 10

Making the final products

The students measure the actual bulletin boards they will be using and finalize their lists of materials. Then they create and put up their bulletin boards.

STEP 11

Celebrating

The group invites others to view their creations at an exhibit.

O P T I O N S

- Most schools have teachers who create especially fine bulletin boards. One option for this project is to invite that teacher to model her or his creative processes for the class.

- Students could create temporary or even permanent murals on school or community walls.

✖ Making It Work in the Classroom

This teacher began most days by having students work in their "sketch books." Simply bunches of plain paper stapled together, the sketch books were places for students to experiment with ideas associated with the theme of their bulletin boards. This sketch time gave the teacher time to set up the many materials needed for this project.

The Field Trip Project

⊗ Overview

The Field Trip Project puts students' field trips into their own hands. Students decide where they want to go and how they are going to get there. They figure out how much it is going to cost, write proposals for money, and make all the necessary arrangements, including making phone calls, writing permission slips, and setting the rules.

⊗ Goal

To go on a field trip!

⊗ Learning Goals for Students

To learn to use a problem-solving strategy.
To learn how to write a persuasive proposal.
To learn how to work together.
To learn proper public behavior.

⊗≋⊗≋⊗≋ The Steps

STEP 1

Introducing the project

The teacher begins by informing students that they will choose, design, and implement their very own field trips. They will brainstorm places to go, critique their ideas, choose one, make all the necessary arrangements, go on the trip, get feedback on their trip, and write an article or brochure about it. All of the steps are outlined, giving students a clear idea of exactly what is going to happen and when.

STEP 2

Deciding on a field trip

Students brainstorm places they would like to go. In small groups, students create lists of pros and cons for several trips. Then they weigh the pros and cons for each trip, and settle on one.

STEP 3

Giving and receiving feedback and revising

Each small group shares their idea for a field trip with the rest of the class, gets feedback, and revises their choice accordingly.

STEP 4

Making arrangements

Students make the necessary phone calls for information about directions, reservations, and costs.

STEP 5

Writing proposals and permission slips

Students create a budget and write a proposal for their field trips. Each proposal must give three good reasons for going on the trip, explain what they will learn, and give a rationale for the budget. Students also write, photocopy, and distribute the permission slips and rules for behavior.

STEP 6

Giving and receiving feedback and revising

The small groups share their proposals with other students and/or the teacher and receive feedback about what works, what doesn't, and how the proposals could be improved. The proposals are revised accordingly and submitted to the office in charge of cash disbursements. This office either funds the trip or ask for more information.

STEP 7

Preparation for and going on the field trip

Each small group provides relevant background information to the class as well as rules of behavior. Then the whole class goes on the field trip.

STEP 8

Discussing the trip

Students (individually or as a class) provide the small group with feedback about their field trip: what they liked, what they didn't like, and what could be done better next time.

STEP 9

Writing brochures or newsletter articles

Students write articles or brochures (some complete with photographs) to tell others about their field trip.

✸ Making It Work in the Classroom

Early in the project, it is important for the teacher to walk the whole class through each step in the problem-solving strategy, which frames the project. After the field trips are decided on, the class has to decide the order of the trips. Usually, in an eight-week period, the first three weeks are devoted to planning. The last five weeks usually have a cycle of going on a field trip, spending a day on feedback and preparation for the next field trip, then the next field trip, and so on. Once the class has taken one trip, the group that planned it begins working on their brochure article and continues working on it throughout the rest of the project.

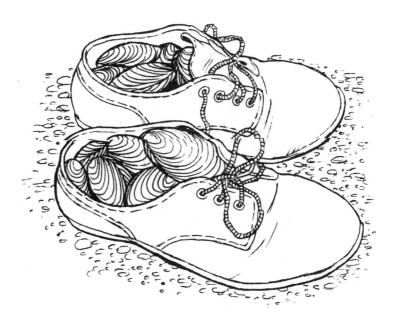

3

Techniques and Strategies
for Teaching Projects

Most teachers respond enthusiastically to the idea of projects but wonder what it will take to make them work in the classroom. This is a valid question: As with any curriculum, a project's success depends on the way it is actually used. And the way the project is used—or "implemented"—in turn, depends in part on the teacher's ability to use teaching techniques appropriate to projects. In this chapter, we discuss several techniques and strategies designed both to make implementing a project more manageable for the teacher and, at the same time, to boost student learning.

These techniques and strategies include:

- Coaching

A coach directs from the sidelines instead of in front of the class. The coach provides support for the students but allows them to take as much responsibility for their own learning as they can.

- Modeling

By observing models, students see how a more experienced person carries out an activity. At times, modeling involves showing students how to do an activity step by step. Teachers, students, and members of the community can be models.

- Ongoing Assessment

Through ongoing assessment, students receive continuous feedback about the quality of their work and how they can improve it.

- Teaching Students How to Think

By focusing on the processes and strategies involved in thinking well, students become more critical, creative, and intelligent.

- Making a Big Deal of Learning Goals

Highlighting your most important goals ensures that students learn what you want them to and gives students the direction they need to practice and improve their skills.

Coaching

> "My role, I believe, is to get [students] started, let them know what our goal is [and] how we want to go about achieving it, . . . get feedback from them, [and] make sure everybody understands their role in the production. Then just take it from there and be able to step back once everybody is doing what they're supposed to be doing and just be there if there are questions from them or if they need guidance."
>
> —*Deb*

What's the Point of Coaching?

The purpose of coaching is to allow students to get the support they need while still giving them the freedom and responsibility to direct their own activities. Like the coach of a sports team, the ultimate goal of a coach in the classroom is to enable students to carry out the work (write an article, manage a budget, and so on) on their own.

What Does a Coach Do?

A coach helps students find activities and problems that present just the right challenge; provides assistance and support when they are needed; and gradually gives each student more and more responsibility for his or her own work.

When Does a Coach Provide Guidance?

Coaches provide assistance when students have trouble getting started or when they appear to be stuck or losing momentum. But they may also offer a quick word of encouragement or ask a brief question of students who have been working effectively on their own for some time. After students have completed a draft or a final piece of work, the coach plays a critical role in helping the students reflect on their work.

An Example of Good Coaching

After the students finished writing in their journals, Dominique handed out the proposals that the students were working on. The proposals described a recipe that the students wanted to make. As the students began to work, she reminded them, "I'm not just going to look at your spelling. These need to be persuasive!"

Most of the children got right to work, even Wallace, Henry, and Kim, who were sitting next to each other and who occasionally had trouble getting started. Dominique noted that Amy was just staring at her paper and went over to ask her how it was going. Amy said she was tired. Dominique asked her what the ingredients were for her recipe and suggested she begin by writing those down. She pointed out that Linda, who was sitting nearby, might be able to help if Amy had any questions. Dominique then moved over to Shamella, who was talking to Pat. Dominique sat down next to Shamella and asked her to read what she had written so far. Dominique pointed out that Shamella needed to think of more reasons to explain why she wanted to make her recipe. She prompted her by asking, "What could you learn by making this? Why would it be better to make this than another recipe?"

When Linda came over to show Dominique her completed proposal, Dominique noted that she had a clear budget and had listed all the steps her group would need to go through to make the recipe. She also remarked that Linda mentioned three good reasons for making the recipe, then asked if she thought it would be easier to understand if she put all the reasons together in one paragraph. Linda nodded and went back to work.

Examples of Coaching Pitfalls and How to Avoid Them

Instead of simply telling Amy to get to work or giving her more help than she really needed, Dominique helped her find an appropriate place to start.

Instead of remaining at the center of the class answering all of the questions herself, Dominique invited students to help each other.

Instead of spending all of her time with one student, Dominique circulated around the room.

Instead of simply instructing Shamella to write more or telling her what additional reasons to write down, Dominique prompted her with questions and encouraged her to come up with more reasons herself.

Instead of telling Linda that she was finished because she had already completed the assignment better than most students, Dominique encouraged her to expand on her work.

How Do You Become a Coach?

There are three essential ingredients to becoming a coach:

- An understanding of what a coach is and what a coach is supposed to do.

- An awareness of the techniques and strategies a coach can use in different situations.

- Practice!

How Can You Better Understand Coaching?

To learn more about coaching, read articles related to coaching; identify examples of effective coaching from your own teaching and learning experiences and compare them to instances in which there was no coaching or coaching was ineffective; think of a lesson you have given in which you were not a coach and imagine what it would have been like if you had acted as one; reflect on your coaching after a class or a project—when were you most effective? When could you have been a better coach? It helps to share your ideas and reflections with your colleagues and others who are familiar with and interested in this approach.

How Does a Coach Interact with Small Groups or Individual Students?

Again, the best coaches give students only as much support as they need. They find the right balance between giving the students no guidance and telling the students what to do. Over the course of a project, they are able to give just the right amount of assistance and advice to each student. Here are a few examples of effective coaching strategies:

- When you identify students who need help, start by giving them only a few hints, then gradually increase your support if the student does not respond.

- Ask simple questions, such as "What do you think you should do first?" or "Can you think of anything else you could do?" Questions like these can help lead students into an activity.

- If students are having trouble, ask them to draw on their own experience for a solution. For example, you might ask, "Have you ever done anything like this before? What did you do?"

- If, after getting a few ideas, a student hasn't started to work, just walk away for a little while, giving the student the chance to do something on her own before you return to check on her.

- If a student is still having trouble, try modeling the activity. Just model a little bit at first, and then, if necessary, model more of the activity.

- As a last resort, if a student still does not understand what to do, it's all right to let him copy what you do—just make sure to ask him to do it again on his own afterward.

Finally, there is no substitute for practice. Over time, coaching will become easier and students will become more used to it. Whenever you can, reflect on your experiences and think about how you can improve your work.

Signs That You Really Are a Coach

- The students spend more time talking than you do.

- You spend more time giving advice and asking questions than giving directions.

- Your enthusiasm for the topic appears to be contagious—students are engaged and interested.

- When students ask for help, you are able to get them to come up with their own ideas about what to do.

- You don't spend large amounts of time working with a single student or group.

- Students gradually become more and more independent.

- When students are stuck, they don't always come to you to get going again.

- You occasionally find yourself with time to stand back and just watch as the students work.

Modeling

> If I were to do a proposal with my class to ask the principal to give us money for a field trip, I think the first proposal I would do . . . on a large piece of paper on the floor with all the kids around me, helping me to write. The best way for [students] to learn is to model what [they're] going to do. I think that's a wonderful way to teach kids.
>
> —Traci

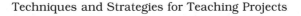

What's the Point of Modeling?

The purpose of modeling is to *show* students the thinking processes that a more expert person goes through when carrying out an activity.

How Does Modeling Work?

Modeling works by giving students a clear idea of what to do and how to do it. They gain a better understanding of the end goal and of the steps they need to go through in order to get there. In addition, when modeling is done well, students get to hear and see how a more expert person thinks and feels about an activity—how she identifies and solves problems, how she makes decisions, why she makes changes and revisions, how she checks on her progress, her enthusiasm about the work, and so on.

When Is Modeling Most Useful?

It is particularly useful to begin activities with just enough modeling to help students think about what they are going to do. Modeling is also helpful when students are stuck or are having particular difficulty. Modeling how a more expert person would solve a similar problem provides students with ideas and assistance while still allowing them to carry out the solution largely on their own. As students become more familiar with an activity, modeling may become less important.

What's the Difference Between Modeling and Giving Examples?

Effective modeling is more than just giving examples. In an example, students are simply shown what to do. For instance, an example of how to make a field-trip proposal might show students what needs to be included in a proposal:

1. A description of where you want to go.

2. A budget that shows how much it will cost.

3. An explanation of why you should be able to go there.

In modeling, however, the teacher demonstrates what she thinks about when carrying out each step of a task. Thus, if the teacher wants to show how she would decide what trip to go on, she might begin by explaining what it means to brainstorm, then brainstorm a list of places to go. She could say, "Brainstorming means getting a lot of ideas out without thinking about whether they are good ideas or not, just being creative and letting your mind think broadly. So let me see, where could we go on a field trip? I'll write them down so I don't forget. We could go to a farm to pick apples or pumpkins. We could go bowling or rollerskating, or to the Science Museum, or the Aquarium, or . . ." After exhausting her own supply of ideas, the teacher would ask students to generate their own lists. Later, she might also demonstrate how she would determine the costs of a trip, explain how she would decide on the strongest and most convincing reasons for the trip, and show how she would ask for and get feedback before turning in her proposal.

Who Can Be an Effective Model?

You need not be the only model available to your students, of course. Anyone—a peer, a teacher, or another person—with more expertise and the ability to explain his or her thinking process can be an effective model. Students can model for each other by simply "thinking out loud." Peer modeling can be particularly helpful to students because the model is likely to be struggling with the same problems or roadblocks that the observing students are experiencing. Bringing those roadblocks into the open for discussion can be very productive.

Inanimate objects can provide effective models too. A poster of the thought processes involved in creating a budget or constructing a sentence can serve as a model, as can other text-based materials. Many new computer programs model skills for students as well. With some creativity, your classroom can provide many models of expert (or near-expert) skills and processes for your students to emulate.

An Example of Effective Modeling

Students are seated at a table and at several desks. Dominique, the teacher, passes out a collection of recipes. She tells the group that they are going to look at the recipes and decide which ones to make.

"But if you want me to get all the ingredients for you, you will have to persuade me, tell me why you want to make these things, and give me a few reasons. And then you will have to give me a budget. Who knows what the word budget means?" Several children raise their hands, and Dominique calls on Laurie. Laurie says it's a certain amount of money. Dominique writes Laurie's answer on the board and says, "That's what we have to figure out: how much money the recipe will cost to make." She writes the instructions on a big piece of paper attached to an easel.

Dominique finishes writing and turns back to the class. "We're going to do a sample budget together." She asks them to turn to the recipe for candy apples. "Let's imagine we are going to make candy apples. In order to figure out how many apples we need, I have to look and see how many people this recipe will feed." She points to the number of servings listed on the recipe and continues, "This recipe is for four people and it calls for four apples. That means that we need one apple for each person. How many people do we need to feed?"

Several students shout out, "Sixteen!" (the number of students in the class plus Dominique), and she nods.

Next, Dominique explains that they will have to estimate how much apples will cost. She asks if anyone has bought any apples at the store. Kim and others raise their hands, and she asks Kim if he remembers how much they cost. He says he thinks they cost about a dollar. "A dollar for how many?" Dominique wonders.

"Three," Kim answers.

"So if we need fifteen apples, I have to get five bunches of three apples. How much will five bunches of three apples cost?" she asks.

"Five dollars!" Wallace announces.

"Right! That's what we're going to have to do for every ingredient."

A Similar Lesson Without Modeling

Dominique might have simply said, "I am going to show you how to do a budget." She would then turn to the blackboard and write:

1. *Figure out how much you need of each ingredient.*

2. *Figure out how much each ingredient costs.*

3. *Multiply the amount by the cost.*

4. *Add up the total.*

In this case, Dominique would have told her students what to do without modeling how to go about it. A lesson like this one is perfectly appropriate sometimes—for instance, when her students are familiar with the processes involved in making budgets and just need a brief reminder. In this case, Dominique doesn't want the group to get bored, so she lets them get started on figuring out the budget on their own. As they work she circulates around the room, and when she sees a student who is having a real problem, she models other parts of the process. In this manner, she keeps the students engaged and gives them a clear idea of what to do.

Some Strategies for Providing Effective Models

One of the best ways to provide good models is to think aloud while you demonstrate the tasks that you want students to learn. Write an essay, solve a math problem, make a decision—do whatever it is your students should be able to do, and do it out loud as they observe. The key here is to be realistic. Learning how to do something right involves learning what to do when things go wrong and you are stuck or confused. Reveal your points of confusion and how you go about resolving them, and your students will learn valuable troubleshooting techniques. Demonstrate how you stand back to see how things are going and fix the parts of your work that aren't quite satisfactory, and your students will learn to reflect on and revise their own work.

Signs That You Are Providing Effective Models

- Your students imitate you.

- Students begin to think aloud themselves and to model for each other.

- Students have a grasp of the processes involved in a task.

- Students troubleshoot when they are stuck, rather than turning immediately to you.

- Students understand how to get started on an activity with which they are unfamiliar.

Ongoing Assessment

Interviewer: Why do you need feedback?

Fourth-Grade Student: Because sometimes I don't [know] what's right, and I need to ask my friends to see if it's right or wrong.

Interviewer: And what do you do with that feedback?

Student: I take the feedback, and then I go back into my story or something, what I'm writing, and then I take out what they say. If it's good, I just leave it. If it's bad, I take it out.

What's the Point of Ongoing Assessment?

One of the basic tenets of the recent trend toward "authentic" or "alternative" assessment is this: Assessment should be a tool for learning. That is, students should be giving and receiving continuous feedback from each other and their teachers about the quality of their work and how they can improve it. Students learn a variety of important lessons from ongoing assessment. They learn to assess and revise their own work, to give and receive constructive criticism, and to produce work that meets the learning goals of the project.

What Are the Key Features of Ongoing Assessment?

Ongoing assessment uses clear criteria against which student work is measured and feedback about how closely students' work comes to meeting those criteria.

How Are Criteria Decided?

In order to judge anything, students must have a clear idea of what counts as good work, so the first step is deciding what the criteria for a project are. There are several ways to set criteria. One way is to simply decide what they are and tell your students. Another is to develop the criteria for a good product or performance in collaboration with your students. A third is to use a combination approach, in which you lay out the broad criteria and the students contribute specifics as they work. The best choice depends largely on your situation, of course, but we encourage you to involve your students in setting criteria whenever you can. They no doubt know a lot about the qualities of good work already, and genuinely involving them in decisions about how their work will be judged tends to result in a deeper understanding of and commitment to the criteria.

There are several ways to determine criteria with students. Some teachers ask their students to brainstorm a list of characteristics of, for example, a good letter, adding their own criteria to the list as needed. They then condense the list and post it on walls, share it with students through handouts, and so on. Others ask students to compare good and not-so-good examples of the given task and draw a list of criteria out of that discussion. Either way, it is important that students understand and accept the criteria they will be expected to meet.

Co-determining criteria with students can be difficult for teachers new to projects. If you are unaccustomed to this kind of activity, we suggest you start simply, and gradually give your students more responsibility as you become more comfortable with your project. Keep the criteria simple at first, and if you don't want to ask your class to determine them, just tell them what they are. As you become more experienced with projects, you can make the criteria more demanding and involve students in decisions about the criteria themselves.

How Is Feedback Given?

So I've taken that feedback aspect of it and have the kids read their stories out loud. And kids don't like to read their stories out loud the first time, the rough draft. They don't want anyone to know what they're saying, but once you get them into it, they do. And they're . . . self-correcting themselves, 'Oops, I spelled this wrong. Oops, this isn't it.' Or someone would say, 'Well, what are you saying here, what happened . . .?' So it's almost like the feedback part of what we do I've implemented to a point where the kids like it.

—Dominique

Once the criteria are set, engaging in ongoing assessment means having students give and receive meaningful feedback about each other's writing, performances, and other work. Again, there are several approaches to take. A popular and effective technique that we have used is feedback sessions. Every few weeks or days, depending on how quickly students work, the teacher coordinates a feedback session in which students discuss each other's work. These sessions follow strict rules: students must comment on the strengths, or what is good about the work, before they air their concerns, or what isn't so good about it; then they recommend improvements. These rules ensure that the feedback sessions are constructive and thoughtful.

In addition to these formal feedback sessions, students receive frequent informal feedback from each other, their teachers, and themselves. Teachers often send students to their peers for feedback and are careful to follow the rules of feedback even when commenting on a child's work on the fly. They also encourage students to give themselves feedback by asking questions such as, "What do you think is good about it? What needs fixing? How will you do that?" rather than automatically giving their own opinions first. Eventually, students begin to reflect on what works, what doesn't, and what can be improved about their work before asking anyone else for their perspective.

An Example of Good Ongoing Assessment

After giving her students a few minutes to wrap up their work, Sabine asks them to join her in the common area for a feedback session. Robin, Ellen, and Nashima volunteer to go first. They perform their anti-violence rap and dance for the group, then take their seats. Sabine asks the group what they think is good about the performance, and a couple of hands shoot up. Raymond notes that the lyrics are good because they mimic a popular song. Francisco compliments the girls on singing clearly and loudly.

After a few more comments, Jane asks, "Can we do bad now?" Sabine gently encourages her to think of it as sharing concerns rather than finding bad things and asks Jane to share her comment and any suggestions for improvement she may have. Jane points out that the dance steps were sloppily done and recommends they either practice them more or make them easier. She jumps up to demonstrate a step she thinks could work. Other students tell the girls that they like the fact that their song is like the popular one, but think it is perhaps too much like it and suggest ways to make the new rap a little more distinctive.

One by one, each group of two or three students gets up and shares their work—a letter to the governor urging him to crack down on drug addicts, a plan to help the homeless, an anti-violence public service announcement. Each group receives thoughtful feedback about how their work measures up to the group's criteria. After the session, Sabine asks everyone to begin revising their work based on the feedback they received.

Examples of Assessment Pitfalls and How to Avoid Them

Instead of simply critiquing her students' work herself and basing her judgments on criteria only she knows, Sabine organized a feedback session.

Rather than allowing students to simply criticize each other's work, Sabine insisted they follow the rules of feedback.

Instead of waiting until students have completed their projects before giving comments or assigning a grade, thereby denying them the opportunity to learn from the assessment and improve their work, Sabine had regular formal and informal feedback sessions as students worked.

Signs That Students Are Using Ongoing Assessment

- Students refer to the criteria when giving and receiving feedback.

- Students use the feedback they get to revise their work.

- Students begin to follow the rules of feedback without being reminded, and catch each other when the rules are being broken.

- Students seek feedback from each other and the teacher spontaneously.

- Students give themselves feedback or reflect on the quality of their work before seeking the opinions of others.

Teaching Students How to Think

All students can think. The point of this section is to show how projects can teach students to think *better*—more carefully, critically, and creatively.

What's the Point of Teaching Students to Think?

Over the past decade or so, educators everywhere have begun to stress the need to teach students how to think as well as how to read, write, remember, calculate, and so on. In fact, when the teaching of thinking is embedded in instruction, students learn basic skills better and become more proficient at them. This is because a large part of learning how to do something is learning the processes and strategies involved in doing it well (this is why modeling one's thinking is an effective teaching tool). For example, good writers use creative and critical thinking moves such as planning, brainstorming, reflection, and revision. An approach to teaching writing that highlights these moves can result in students who write better and who are better creative and critical thinkers in general.

What Are the Key Features of Teaching Students to Think?

There are lots of ways to teach thinking. Many approaches revolve around a thinking framework or strategy.

What Is a Thinking Strategy?

A thinking strategy is a collection of thinking steps that help people accomplish a task in a thoughtful and intelligent way. Such strategies often reflect what experts or good thinkers do when they think through a task. The writing process briefly referred to above is one example. A second example of a thinking strategy is a decision-making strategy that asks students to brainstorm options, list the pros and cons for several promising options, weigh the pros and cons, and make a careful choice. Students are likely to make better, more creative decisions by following the steps of a decision-making strategy like this one.

The critical and creative power of such a strategy can be boosted even more by connecting criteria, or rules, to each step. These criteria are intended to guide students in just how to think when doing the step. For example, the rules of brainstorming are: think broadly, get all ideas on the table, and do not critique any ideas until the next step (which is to list pros and cons). The rules of listing pros and cons are: critique all ideas fairly by seeking cons as well as pros for favorite options and vice versa, and look for different kinds of pros and cons, including hidden ones.

The Smart Thinking strategy referred to throughout this guidebook is a third example of a thinking strategy. The Smart Thinking strategy came about one summer when we discovered that each of our projects presented students with design problems to solve. Organizing a field trip, fighting homelessness, saving the earth, planning refreshments for a party, and creating a newspaper or a game can all be seen as complex tasks that require students to design a solution or a product. We decided to make a "big deal" of teaching thinking by creating one problem-solving strategy that could be used in each project. Our strategy, called "Smart Thinking," is displayed on pages 10–11. This strategy encourages teachers and students to approach projects in a thoughtful and stepwise way and to avoid the pitfalls of hasty thinking by following the "Smart Rules" associated with the steps of the strategy.

An Example of How To Use a Thinking Strategy

The Bulletin Board Project uses the Smart Thinking process as a framework. Deb, the teacher, begins by explaining the goals and processes of the project. She has a large poster of the Smart Thinking strategy on the wall, which she uses to outline the steps of the project. After this brief overview, she has her students **get background information** *about bulletin boards. She takes them on a tour of the school and asks them to look at* various bulletin boards and think about what makes the good ones good. Back in the classroom, they list the characteristics of the good bulletin boards.

After the tour, Deb reminds students that the next step in the process involves **deciding on the purpose** of their boards. "What do you want your bulletin boards to do?" she asks. "What is the point of making them?" Several children say they want their boards to send messages like "Stay in school" or "Don't do drugs." Others want their boards to "just look like art" or explore their African roots. One student wants to showcase the latest fashions. Deb encourages them to choose one purpose as the most important goal for every bulletin board they make, but they cannot happily settle on one. In the spirit of flexibility, Deb agrees that students can choose different purposes, as long as each board has a clear purpose.

The group eventually chooses two purposes—sending a message and exploring African roots. Deb then asks them to **brainstorm** a list of compelling topic ideas for each purpose. As they offer ideas, Deb is careful to see that they follow the rules of brainstorming and reminds them to think creatively. She has to ask them several times to refrain from commenting on ideas, but they eventually get the hang of it.

When they seem to have run out of ideas, Deb tells them to get into their small working groups and **carefully select the best idea** by listing the pros and cons of a few of the most interesting ideas. Through discussion and debate, each group settles on one topic for their board.

Over the next few days, students **make a first version** of their board. Actually, they make several "first" versions, in which they test out ideas by drawing page-sized mock-ups of their boards. When they feel they have found one they can work with, they tell Deb that they are ready for feedback. They **get feedback** from each other and their teacher in formal feedback sessions. Deb insists that the feedback refers explicitly to the list of qualities that make up a good bulletin board that they generated during the Get Information step early in the project.

After getting feedback, students are given opportunities to **make revisions** and improve upon their work. When they are ready, they arrange a public **exhibition** of their work.

How Do You Use a Thinking Strategy in a Project?

The most straightforward way to use a strategy like Smart Thinking is to build your project around it from the start, like Deb did. That is, have students begin by collecting information, then have them brainstorm ideas around whatever task or problem they are working on, and so on. The benefits of this approach include the flexible backbone, or framework, that the strategy provides for the project and the clear processes that it provides for the students.

Many projects are not quite that straightforward, however. In fact, we have found that very few projects progress directly through the Smart Thinking strategy step by step. Rather, they may begin at the beginning, move a step or two into the strategy, then curve back around again and start over before reaching the end. Or, a project may reflect a "grab bag" approach, in which certain steps of the strategy are used as needed by the class. For example, brainstorming is particularly useful when students need to come up with ideas about what to do, so a lot of brainstorming goes on at different points in different projects. Although it is important for students to see how each step of a strategy hangs together with the others, it is not necessary to be rigid in how you use these steps.

Signs That Students Are Learning to Think Well

- Students use the terms of the strategy spontaneously.

- Students remind each other to follow the rules of the strategy steps.

- Students take time to engage in steps such as feedback or revision that they had overlooked before.

- Student work is more thoughtful and creative.

- Students tend to stand back and ask themselves whether they are going about a task properly; that is, whether they are using the strategy and if so, if they are using it well.

Making a Big Deal of Learning Goals

Making a big deal of your learning goals simply means focusing on and repeatedly emphasizing a select set of the most important skills and concepts you hope to teach.

What's the Point of Emphasizing Learning Goals?

There are few things that can be learned adequately after one or two tries, even if the skill or concept is coached, modeled, assessed, and thought smartly about. Just as practice makes a tremendous difference to athletes, multiple experiences with a particular skill or concept are essential to students. The main purpose of making a big deal of a few learning goals, then, is to give your students many opportunities to achieve them. Related purposes include helping students recognize what they have learned and are now capable of doing and helping them transfer what they learn to contexts outside of your project, your classroom, and your school.

What If Teachers Do Not Emphasize Learning Goals?

Even when teachers do not make a big deal out of a project's learning goals, students may still learn something. However, they are unlikely to learn as efficiently or as deeply as they could, they are unlikely to know the value of what they have learned, and they may not recognize the progress they are making. Finally, students will rarely connect what they have learned to other contexts if teachers do not emphasize a few learning goals.

How Do You Make a Big Deal of Learning Goals?

Making a big deal of learning goals involves doing two things: (1) choosing the learning goals to emphasize and (2) giving students repeated opportunities to work toward those goals in a variety of contexts. The first step asks you to focus on some of the "higher order" learning goals you have for your students—those important goals that can apply to different tasks and disciplines. Thinking strategically; seeing things from different points of view; thinking critically; analyzing, interpreting, and synthesizing new information; and collaborating are just a few examples of higher order learning goals. Picking one or two such goals to focus on is a critical first step.

The second step is to work activities and instructional episodes related to your higher order goals into your curriculum or project as often as possible. Be careful to do this in a way that will not bore your students, or the project will no longer seem genuine to the group.

Each of the first four techniques discussed in this chapter can also contribute to making a big deal of most learning goals. For example, "persuasive writing" was one of the central learning goals in the Mather Afterschool Program. We used coaching techniques to guide students through the writing process. We used modeling techniques to demonstrate writing. We used ongoing assessment, including frequent feedback sessions, to teach students about the criteria for good persuasive writing. And we taught them to use the Smart Thinking strategy to make their writing more thoughtful and creative. Taken together, these four techniques helped us make a big deal of persuasive writing in each of our projects.

How Can You Emphasize Learning Goals Across Projects?

Making a big deal of your learning goals within a project is essential to student learning. Even better, however, is emphasizing the same goals across projects. When students encounter the same learning goals in project after project, the chances of improvement in their skills and understanding will skyrocket.

The effect can't seem redundant to students, however. If there is not enough variety in the tasks, or the activities do not fit naturally into the projects, students are likely to become weary of what they see as "the same old thing." For this reason, we have found it useful to embed our central learning goals into projects in different ways. For example, the Cooking Project engages students in writing persuasively for the money they need to cook, the Business Project has students write persuasively for loans and about what should be done with the profits from their sales, and the Field Trip Project has them write proposals for places to go. These may not strike you as remarkably diverse tasks or contexts, but it is enough to keep our students writing.

Here are three additional techniques that are especially useful in helping teachers make a big deal of learning goals across projects:

- Using key words.

- Emphasizing common and explicit rules, steps, or frameworks.

- Making diagrams that describe your approach.

Using key words. By identifying and frequently using a few key terms, teachers can quickly and efficiently signal to students that they are involved in an activity related to the learning goals. For example, "feedback" and "brainstorming" are two terms that we use often in each project. Teachers label feedback and brainstorming sessions as such, and posters with these terms hang in every classroom. This way, students encounter the same terms and phrases across contexts. The result is that they get the repeated exposure and practice necessary for them to learn.

Emphasizing common and explicit frameworks. Again, having rules, steps, or strategies common to multiple contexts can really boost student learning. This is why, in spite of the surface differences between each of our projects, we put together one thinking strategy that can be used in each project. Encountering the Smart Thinking strategy in project after project helps our students know what to expect (clear goals and processes) and makes a big deal of learning to think well.

Making diagrams that describe your approach. Graphic organizers such as diagrams and pictures that represent learning goals serve as reminders of how students should approach activities. For example, when we ask students to brainstorm, we can point to a poster on the wall that reminds them of the rules to follow. Similarly, our symbol for brainstorming—a cloud with thunderbolts—can be placed in journals and other materials to indicated times when brainstorming might be appropriate. When all teachers use the same diagrams and pictures, their teaching is more effective.

Signs That You Have Successfully Emphasized Your Learning Goals

- Students know what the learning goals are.

- Key terms are commonly used by teachers and students.

- Posters and other graphic organizers are visible and referred to frequently.

- Students attend to the rules, steps, or frameworks without having to be reminded.

- Students are learning!

Although we have listed the five techniques for making projects work for learning separately—coaching, modeling, ongoing assessment, teaching thinking, and making a big deal of learning goals—they are closely connected. Part of being a good coach, for example, is knowing when to model an activity and when it is time to let students continue on their own. Modeling can help students learn how to brainstorm or give feedback. Assessing students' use of thinking strategies by making the criteria for good thinking clear and giving feedback that helps them recognize when they are and are not meeting those criteria is an excellent way to teach thinking. There are times when particular techniques can be especially powerful, but in general, these are not techniques that have to be used one at a time or in a strict sequence. They are tools that can be used in combination to ensure that your students get the most out of every project.

4

Designing a Good Project

The previous chapter laid the foundation for a good project—genuineness, clear goals and processes, flexibility, a natural context for learning, and student self-direction. This chapter is intended to guide you in designing your own project in a thoughtful and reflective way. We begin by telling the story of the evolution of one teacher's project over the course of three years, illustrating the key challenges she faced and the ways in which she handled them. Then we go on to outline how you can design a successful project.

The Evolution of a Project: One Teacher's Experience

The Cooking Project started out as the Snack Project. The original idea was to let students choose which snacks were served at the afterschool program. Their decision-making process involved reading food labels, testing popular snack foods for fat and sugar content, and taking a survey of children's snack preferences.

We chose the Snack Project for two reasons. We knew most students love food, and learning about nutrition presented an opportunity to develop thinking skills such as comparing and contrasting, making predictions, and estimating. In other words, we believed a Snack Project would be genuinely meaningful and motivating to students and provide a natural context for important learning goals as well.

Although the project got off to a good start, we soon ran into a genuineness problem. Once the initial novelty wore off, the experiments seemed pointless to the students: They knew what they wanted for snack, and they didn't have to do a series of experiments to figure it out.

As the students lost focus, we became more and more concerned with engaging them in a genuinely meaningful project goal. The second and third times we did the project, the goal was to select and prepare food for a party for the entire afterschool program. That was *very* genuine. Everyone was excited about it, and we figured cooking would give us a chance to focus on fractions and measurement as well as nutrition and thinking skills.

As the party drew nearer, however, we found that food preparation had become more central to our students than many of our most important learning goals. Students were very interested in chopping tomatoes and slicing fruit, but not in learning about nutrition or how to think strategically. Even fractions and measurement got less attention than we had hoped, because we used very simple recipes. Although the students had a good time, they did not learn as much as we had wanted them to.

We needed to find a better balance between genuineness and learning. Our challenge for the second year was to find a way to make learning goals a more natural part of the project. We knew we wanted to teach writing, thinking skills, and collaboration, and making a group cookbook seemed to be the perfect way to accomplish this. Students would need to plan, to test and evaluate recipes, to write about their recipes, and to produce a group product.

Although we were excited about the idea, we discovered that cookbooks were not as interesting to our students, many of whom had never even seen one before. Because our third-through fifth-grade students did not need or want cookbooks, we had run into another genuineness problem.

We were stumped. We just couldn't seem to find a natural context for teaching students to write better in the Cooking Project. We met with the other teachers in the program and asked their advice. Carol, the teacher of the Field Trip Project, suggested we borrow an idea from her project and have kids write proposals before they cooked. It was perfect! Not only would it provide a natural context for writing, but it would require that students reason and think critically as well.

The next term, we told students that they were going to cook, but that they had to write proposals telling us what they wanted to make, why they wanted to make it, and how much it would cost. These proposals would be "funded" only when they met the standards for a good proposal. Once a proposal was funded, cooking would begin. Our students have been happily writing (and reasoning, giving feedback, and cooking) ever since.

Project Design Is an Ongoing Process

Don't let the story about the Cooking Project mislead you—we didn't stop improving it, and the balance between genuineness and learning was not the only challenge to making it work. We continued to fine-tune the project during the third and fourth years of the program. For instance, we experimented with co-creating the standards for a good proposal with students. We found that discussing the differences between a good proposal and a mediocre one gave them a reason to work harder, to seek and give feedback about the quality of their work, and to revise, so this activity became a permanent part of the project.

We are happy now with the balance we have managed to strike between fun and learning, but making the goal of the project more genuine while providing a good reason for writing well and thinking carefully were not the only things that contributed to its development. Finding the right materials, figuring out how much time it took for students to complete each activity, familiarizing students with classroom routines, and becoming comfortable with the teaching techniques appropriate to projects (coaching, modeling, and so on; see Chapter 3) were all important elements of our success. This all took time, including time to reflect, time to talk with other teachers, and time to plan improvements.

The moral of the story, then, is "persistence pays." Perhaps the best advice we can offer to the teacher new to projects is to keep evaluating and experimenting with a project and the teaching techniques that make it work. The project design process described below will get you started.

How to Design Your Own Project

Designing a project thoughtfully and carefully involves first choosing and planning a project, and then continuing to try it out, reflect on how it went, revise it, and try it again, until the project works well for you and your students. The process recommended here explains each of these steps. It may appear a bit cumbersome at first, but we encourage you to try it anyway, because it reflects our experience and our knowledge of how best to avoid the obstacles associated with making the switch to projects.

Picking a Project

Picking a project goal is a critical first step when planning a project. This feels a little backward to some teachers, many of whom are used to thinking about learning goals—abstract objectives like "understanding" and "appreciating"—before deciding on project goals—the concrete products or performances that result from students' work, such as a book or a newspaper or a field trip. It is important that the goals or events you build your project around be meaningful to and understood by you and your students, so the first step in our planning process is to think about what students will produce.

We have found that one of the challenges involved in picking a project goal and turning it into a project is finding a balance between the need for *genuineness* and the need for a *natural context for learning*. Project ideas often start out overemphasizing one or the other. Thinking broadly as well as critically about the possibilities for your project can help you create a balance between these two key characteristics right from the start. Here is the planning process we recommend:

1. Begin by brainstorming a list of potentially genuine project goals or culminating events. Your chances of coming up with a good, genuine project are better if you cast a wide net at this point, so be creative—you will narrow the list down later.

2. List *all* of your learning goals. Be sure to include learning goals that are important but often neglected, such as the ability to think critically, as well as goals that are particularly appropriate to projects, like the ability to be organized and make plans, or to collaborate. Again, think broadly about what you want to teach, because you will narrow the list down later.

3. Pick three of the most promising project goals from your first list.

4. Use a graphic organizer like the one on the next page (or whatever method works best for you) to sketch out one of the projects.

Making a Sketch of Your Project Goals and Activities

Culminating Event: *Business Project*

Sketch the goals and activities of the project using a curriculum map. The circles in the center should represent the goals of the project, or the concrete products and performances students are working toward. The outlying circles should contain possible activities—the work students will engage in to reach the goals. Write the kinds of learning that can result from each activity next to the activity circles, as we have done in italics.

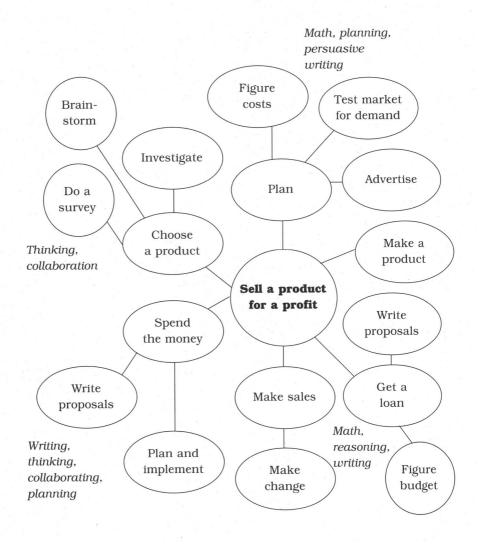

5. After completing a sketch of a project, use the guidelines on the next page to help you think critically about the degree to which it is genuine and provides natural contexts for your learning goals.

6. Sketch a second project to consider, even if you are relatively happy with your first sketch. Pushing yourself to think further at this point is one way to boost your creativity and ensure that you end up with the best possible project.

   Evaluate each of your new sketches as before, using the guidelines for genuineness and for determining whether your project provides a natural context for learning.

7. Pick a project to implement by comparing your sketches. The one that rated highest on both sets of guidelines is probably your best bet.

Evaluating Your Project Sketches

Use these guidelines to evaluate your project sketch in terms of genuineness and the degree to which it provides a natural context for learning.

	Needs work	**Better**	**Good**
Genuine	The project lacks concrete products or performances; OR many goals and activities are unlikely to be engaging to me or to my students.	The goals and some of the activities are motivating, but some may seem forced or irrelevant (i.e., writing essays just for the sake of writing).	The goals of the project are likely to be interesting and meaningful, and the relevance of each activity to those goals is clear.
Provides a natural context for learning	The project emphasizes fact and skill acquisition over working toward a genuine goal; OR it emphasizes fun and does not accommodate learning goals.	The project comfortably accommodates one or two important learning goals, but neglects others.	Reaching the goals of the project requires that students develop important skills and under-standings. Most or all activities accommodate the learning goals.

Planning a Project

1. Your project sketch probably includes many potential learning goals. Decide which learning goals to make a "big deal" of by picking two or three of the most important and appropriate learning goals (See pages 81–84 for a discussion about making a big deal of learning goals). You can still have other objectives, of course, but these will be the ones you stress and give students multiple opportunities to work toward.

2. Sketch out your chosen project in more detail, using whichever planning methods you prefer (See pages 89–91 for one approach to writing up a project).

3. Get feedback from your colleagues on what they think the potential strengths and weaknesses of your project are, as well as any suggestions for improvement they can offer.

4. Revise the project according to the feedback.

Improving Your Projects over Time

1. Try the project with your students. Reflect with and without them on what works, what doesn't work, and what you might do differently next time. Take notes on page 95.

2. Take time to reflect on your project by reviewing your notes.

3. Use the guidelines on page 96 to evaluate the overall success of the project.

4. Revise the project.

5. Try it again! Continue this cycle of planning, implementation, reflection, and revision until the end of time or until you retire, whichever comes first.

Reflecting on Your Project

As you implement your project, take brief notes on what worked well, what didn't, and what you might do differently next time. Refer to the five characteristics of a good project as you reflect. Use these notes at the end of the project to help you revise it.

What went well:

What did not go well:

What to do differently next time:

Reflecting on Your Project

After trying all or part of the project with your students, use this chart to reflect on how it went.

	Needs work	Better	Good
The project was of genuine interest	Both the students and I lost interest, and the project lost momentum.	Interest wavered, but we managed to keep moving toward the goal.	Both the students and I remained interested in the project.
The project provided a natural context for learning	Learning and fun were separate.	Several activities need to be integrated better with the goals of the project.	Learning and fun went hand-in-hand.
The project had clear goals and processes	Students often lost sight of what they were working toward and how what they were doing related to that goal.	The goals were clear, but students were often unsure of what they should be doing.	Students knew the goal(s) of the project and what they needed to do to get there.
The project was flexible	There was one project goal, and all students did the same work at approximately the same time.	There were a few different goals and activities, but several opportunities to capitalize on student interests were missed.	The project encompassed a variety of goals and allowed students to approach them according to their talents and interests.
The project encouraged self-direction	I stood at the front of the room and talked students through most activities.	I tended to address the entire class less frequently, but could probably do so even less. (See Chapter 2 for a discussion of teaching techniques that support student self-direction.)	Students worked in groups or independently while I moved about the room and acted as a coach much of the time.

What can you do to improve your project?

Teaching Through Projects

5

Teaching Through Projects: Challenge and Promise

Gwynne: What advice would you give to a teacher new to projects?

Traci: I would just basically cite examples from my own experience to explain to them in detail what it was like and how everything wasn't always hunky-dory, that we fell down a couple of times before we were able to ride off into the sunset, that it was trial and error. And who knows, maybe this person has a wonderful idea that's going to work well with them and their students but . . . let them know that it's OK . . . if it doesn't work out the first time, . . . that sometimes you're going to learn [through making mistakes] what works best for you and your students.

Sometimes, no matter how worthy a new approach, the transition from one way of teaching to another can be rocky. Our conversations with teachers about what is involved in learning to "do projects" have revealed certain challenges particular to this approach. Not surprisingly, we found that many of the difficulties revolved around what makes projects distinctive—their genuineness, the need to find a natural context for learning, and so on. In this chapter we discuss how these challenges arose as a natural outcome of the teachers' developing expertise with the project method, and we share their advice on how to negotiate these challenges successfully.

To varying degrees, teachers encounter three common challenges when learning to use the project approach in their classrooms:

- Developing a clear conception of the goals and steps of their projects.

- Creating natural contexts for learning.

- Acquiring skill and ease with self-directed learning and related teaching strategies.

In this chapter, we describe how the teachers from the Mather School experienced and negotiated each of these challenges.

The Challenge: Defining Your Goals and Steps

> To tell you the truth, I didn't really have a goal at the beginning of the year. . . . I didn't have any goals because I didn't know what to expect.
>
> —*Uyen Chi*

It's only natural that, never having done projects before, teachers new to this approach are uncertain about what exactly a project is and how it might play itself out in the classroom. Teachers' uncertainty often results in their having difficulty determining a genuine and concrete goal for a project, and their feeling vague about how students will reach that goal. Fortunately, teachers tend to be used to this kind of uncertainty and bravely experiment with new ideas and approaches in spite of it.

In the case of a project-based approach, however, having a clear conception of how the project will proceed is critical. This is true for several reasons. We argued in Chapter 1 that in order for a project to work it needs to be genuinely interesting and motivating to students. Clear project goals provide a "hook," or a way to motivate students, that projects with vague or abstract goals lack. We also argued in Chapter 1 that in order for students to be self-directed they need to understand the goals and processes of the project, or what they are working toward and how they can get there. When a teacher's conception of both the goals and processes are unclear, it is very hard to make the point of the project clear to students.

The problem then is the potential for a lack of both interest and self-direction on the part of the students. Fortunately, with time and experience, coming up with clear, genuine goals and making those goals clear to students becomes easier.

How Do I Identify a Genuine Project with a Clear Goal?

[A project has to be] something that you're really into. I always think about the example with [another teacher]. Even though the playground project was a wonderful project, . . . she just couldn't get with it. It just wasn't her. But [the next time] she found something that . . . was important to her, and that's when her project soared.

—Dominique

Making a project genuinely meaningful and interesting to both the teacher and the students can be trickier in a regular classroom than in an afterschool or other out-of-school program, but in many ways the challenge is the same in any setting. Finding a topic that is particularly interesting to you is a good place to start, as Dominique's remark reveals.

Unfortunately, however, you can't take for granted that what is genuine to you will also be genuine to your students. For example, the teacher referred to by Dominique always wanted to include classical music in her classroom activities but could never find the time. Given the opportunity to design a project in the afterschool program, she considered a focus on baroque music. Although baroque music certainly has potential as a project, we (the authors and more experienced teachers) advised her to start out with something that was more likely to appeal to her particular students, and to strive to come up with a concrete goal for her project—something beyond the "understanding" and "appreciating" learning goals typical of traditional instruction. We encouraged her to ask some hard questions: "Is this a topic that the third-, fourth-, and fifth-grade students know anything about? Is it likely to be one in which they have any interest? Is there any exciting, concrete product that they can take away from this project?"

In our discussions, we came up with ideas for music projects—like writing pieces of music in the baroque style—that had concrete goals that we thought would be more interesting and relevant for the students, but they seemed too demanding. This teacher eventually discarded the idea of doing a project focused on baroque music and went on to brainstorm a whole list of projects that might provide a better fit between her own and her students' interests.

Our advice to you, then, is to follow this teacher's lead by thinking broadly and creatively about a number of different projects before settling on one. Then think carefully about potential concrete goals for a few of the projects that sound most interesting. As many of our teachers have discovered, it's the goal that makes a project meaningful, not just the topic. As you think about the goals of your potential projects, ask yourself what appeals to you about them—what "turned you on" about them: For instance, "learning about rocks and minerals" can sound pretty dry and boring, but polishing rocks and making jewelry is a project with a concrete goal that motivates students. By capitalizing on the appeal of jewelry, studying rocks and minerals becomes more meaningful to your students.

Thinking through a couple of projects in this way can help you to come up with goals that will really motivate your students. You can also talk to *them* about their interests. You might ask your students to join you in brainstorming a list of projects that you can narrow down and choose from later. Don't forget your colleagues and even your own children too. Many of them may have some experience with interesting projects and might be able to give you some useful feedback about the genuineness of your goals.

Finally, you can always boost the genuineness of less-than-thrilling projects by infusing them with goals that you *know* students want to achieve. We have found that when goals like making food, going on field trips, and/or earning money are incorporated into a project *in a meaningful way* (that is, not just as a reward for doing the other, boring stuff) they provide powerful incentives for our students and add a healthy dose of genuineness to the project. In fact, recognizing the motivational power of money, food, and field trips is how we came up with the Business, Cooking, and Field Trip projects.

What If My Project Goals Turn Out Not to Be Genuine Anyway?

If you run into a "genuineness problem" anyway, there are several things you can do. First, it may be that students need a reminder about the goals and their significance. Even if students are interested in making jewelry, they may not be motivated to learn about different kinds of rocks and minerals unless they understand that what they learn will help them to make their own rings and necklaces. Second, be prepared to make changes large and small in your project. That sounds scary, but if you talk to your students about what they like and don't like about the project and are willing to capitalize on their interests as they arise, you are likely to experience what the teacher referred to above experienced—you may have a project that suddenly takes off.

How Do I Make the Goals and Steps Clear to My Students?

Once you have developed a meaningful goal and created a flexible plan or map of the routes your project can take, the next challenge is to get this information across to your students clearly and concisely. Here are a few techniques that teachers commonly use to ensure that the goals and processes of their projects are clear to the students:

- Tell them! Never underestimate the importance of informing students of what you have planned for them and how everything they do ties in with that plan.

- Having a poster or some other visual aid to refer to can be invaluable. For an example of one kind of visual aid representing the steps of a project, see the "Smart Thinking" graphics on pages 10–11.

- Having daily agendas that outline a day's activities can also help. See page 19 for a sample agenda.

- Some teachers make their projects' goals more concrete by sharing models—usually work done by past students (real or imaginary).

- It is important to review with your students the goal(s) and the steps at several points throughout the project.

What if I Fail to Make the Goals and Steps Clear?

With the first group that came in, I don't think they really had a clear-cut idea of what they were doing . . . . Maybe because I felt like I didn't know where it was going either, . . . I was just doing it day by day and just hoping that eventually it [would] get better.

—Uyen Chi

If you feel that you floundered through your project unable to see where you were headed, don't despair. As the teacher quoted at the beginning of this chapter said, things aren't always "hunky-dory" the first time around, but it gets better. The next time you'll have your previous experience to draw on, you'll have some examples of the students' work to share with students when talking about the goals of the project, and you'll be better able to take advantage of the tips listed on page 103. As you try out different projects or carry out one project for the second or third time, you will gain the experience you need to know when to clarify the goals of the project and when to adjust or expand them.

The Challenge:
Creating Natural Contexts for Learning

[Projects] are a wonderful way to get kids to be creative and work on their academic skills and yet [have] fun. . . . For example, I'm doing a 'Cultural Celebration' project and we're talking about cultures. Yet my kids write almost every day, and they're going to be revising their letters that they've been writing to their pen pals. And those kids don't have to say, 'Well, we're doing schoolwork,' because they don't know—because it's sort of masked or we've made it so that kids are having fun and they're learning at the same time.

—Traci

Perhaps the most challenging aspect of a project approach is creating a natural context for learning. Whether in school or after school, many teachers are likely to emphasize either fun or learning rather than plan activities that incorporate both. This can cause one of two problems in a project: Without a natural context for learning, you may find that (1) the learning goals "drop out" of your project as you strive to provide students with a genuine goal (remember what happened with the Cooking Project on page 87, or (2) the level of student engagement and self-direction plummets when the learning goals become forced and their relation to the project goal is either ill-suited or unclear.

One common example of an "unnatural" context for learning is the class that is put into groups because it is good for them to learn to work with others, not because working in groups is the best way to accomplish the goals of the project. Children tend to enjoy working in small groups, but if the task doesn't lend itself to group work, this tactic may backfire. Although it would be easy to conclude that students don't know how to work together, it could be that they are responding to the lack of a match between the goal and the approach.

How Do I Create Natural Contexts for Learning?

The first few steps of the planning process recommended in Chapter 4 address the need to balance fun and learning. Not surprisingly then, we advise you to plan a project the way we've outlined there. In this way, you will ensure that the tasks students are asked to engage in make sense in terms of the goals of the project. Here are a few more tips for finding natural contexts for your learning goals:

- Almost any project can become educational if students are given responsibility for most or even all of it. For example, going on a field trip may seem like an educationally barren event at first, but if you think about what needs to be done to plan the trip, it is actually quite involved. Often, our mistake is in making adults responsible for things like information gathering, problem solving, budgeting, shopping, and getting permissions. When we hand these responsibilities over to the children, going on a field trip becomes a context rich with learning opportunities. Scour your project for opportunities like those in the Field Trip Project—tasks that demand intellectual work of your students and that make sense in terms of the goals of the project as well.

- When implementing your project, make the relevance of the tasks clear to your students. Just as with the need to create clear goals and processes, the momentum of a project depends, in part, on whether or not students "get" what they are doing and why. They need to understand why writing proposals, creating budgets, and collecting information are all vital aspects of their project. Take the time to explain it to them and show them how it worked for other students, if possible.

- If and when you find you have included a task in your project that simply doesn't fit well, the obvious solution is to drop it. However, it may be related to learning goals that are important or even mandatory. If this is the case, you might try to make your project fit the task, rather than the other way around. For example, it was important for students in the Business Project to write. Getting a loan involved some persuasive writing, but only a few children were involved in that task. To get each child to write, Deb decided to have everyone write a proposal for how the profits from their sale should be spent. In this way, she made her project fulfill her learning goals in a way that felt natural and made sense to her students.

The Challenge:
Learning to Help Students Be Self-Directed

Heidi: What is difficult about doing projects?

Deb: Personally, having to pull away from my teacher [perspective on] how I think a classroom should be run or how I was taught when I was a kid, and the residue left from that . . . . [I have] to be able to cross over into allowing the kids a little bit more freedom in expression, a little bit more freedom in helping develop things as they go along.

Simply put, most teachers aren't trained to coach, they are trained to lead. Working in a self-directed classroom, therefore, often requires an adjustment from traditional classroom roles for both the teacher and students. Initially, many teachers tend to retain classroom control, directing rather than facilitating student work. Students, in turn, initially tend to continue to look to the teacher for step-by-step directions and to wanderaimlessly when it isn't forthcoming. It is nearly impossible to get a project off the ground when this is the case.

This problem has led some teachers to conclude that students simply cannot manage their own academic work. Not true! It can work. The challenge is to (1) Learn how to promote student self-direction, and (2) Get students used to being self-directed.

How Can My Teaching Style
Promote Student Self-Direction?

I'm used to teaching one direct way, and I brought that to the afterschool program when I worked with kids. And at first, I didn't think I was effective. So now I'm switching. And it's effective too, so now I know . . . . I've gotten accustomed to letting learning be more free for them.

—Dominique

Being flexible and using teaching techniques such as coaching and modeling will give students the opportunity to work independently. Teachers experienced in the project approach act as coaches by modeling the thinking involved in a particular learning activity, by supporting students' independent or small-group work, and by encouraging reflection on student work in feedback sessions. See Chapter 3 for a discussion of each of these techniques and Chapter 1 for advice about being flexible.

Here is one rather unusual piece of advice for the teacher-as-coach in the self-directed classroom: Be prepared to let your students fumble around, make mistakes, and take twice as long as it would take you to get something done. As their coach, your job is not to do a task for them, but rather to show them how to do something (model), to let them try it themselves, to give them feedback on their performance if necessary (sometimes it's very clear when they mess up!), and to guide them in figuring out what they need to do differently the next time they try it. They may be less efficient than you would be, but they will learn!

How Do I Help My Students Become More Comfortable with Self-Direction?

The first time [I tried the project, the students looked at me] like, 'What do we have to do ?' But the third time around, I didn't get, 'What do you want me to do?' [Instead] they knew what they were doing.

— Sabine

Most students are accustomed to teacher-directed classrooms. Consequently, they require supportive routines, as well as clearly defined steps and processes, to guide them through a project. This section suggests approaches to classroom management and to helping individual students that allow you to be more of a coach and to give your students more control over their work. Classroom management techniques that are critical to supporting self-directed learning are:

- Consistent classroom routines.

- Clear roles and responsibilities for students.

- A supportive physical layout of the classroom.

Consistent classroom routines. Students generally respond positively to being coached if they are given enough guidance to keep them on track. One almost transparent way to provide such guidance is by establishing consistent classroom routines. In any classroom setting, daily routines are established in the first weeks of school as children become familiar with day-to-day activities and the timing of these events in the course of the day and week.

For example, in the Newspaper Project, every day begins the same way—with journal writing. Students know this by the second week of the program and head straight for their journals upon entering the classroom. After writing quietly for ten minutes or so, they return their journals to the shelf and turn their attention to their teacher, Traci, who leads a brief group meeting. She hands out copies of the day's agenda, answers any questions, then has students break into small groups and work independently for the rest of the day. Traci goes from group to group, providing guidance where it is needed. This consistency in classroom routine extends to the end of the day as well. Each day wraps up with time for cleanup and small rewards for good work.

These routines let students know what to expect and what is expected of them at any given point in time and frees them up to be more self-directed than they could otherwise be. Having a classroom full of self-directed students, in turn, allows the teacher to act as a coach, because students are not relying on her to tell them what to do from moment to moment.

Clear roles and responsibilities. As self-directed learners under the guidance of a coach, students assume roles different from those in more traditional classroom settings, where they often sit and wait for the teacher's directions or even permission before they can move ahead on an activity. The creation of specific classroom roles can help students assume greater responsibility for their learning and allow the teacher to coach rather than command. Whenever possible, we favor allowing students to choose their roles by volunteering.

Again, the Newspaper Project provides a telling illustration. As reporters, students are responsible for choosing a topic, writing a draft, and entering the story into the computer. These tasks involve a series of responsibilities, which are made explicit to the students by a daily list of tasks as well as a planning sheet that Traci reviews with the group. In addition, students volunteer for or are assigned roles as photographers, editors, layout editors, and/or distributors of the newspaper.

A classroom layout that supports student self-direction. The arrangement of classroom furniture and the accessibility of materials can hinder or encourage student self-direction. If desks and chairs are arranged in rows facing the front of the room, this implies that students should also be facing the front of the room, listening to the teacher, and working alone. In a self-directed classroom where students are often engaged in a variety of activities at once, the furniture and space should be arranged in ways that support small-group work as well as occasional large-group activities. A clearly defined large-group area (whether it be a central table or a carpeted section of the room), distinct work spaces for individual or small-group work, and clear pathways among the separate areas support the kind of focused, cooperative work characteristic of projects.

Traci's room, for example, has separate spaces for each of the different kinds of activities that go on in the Newspaper Project, including an area for large-group meetings where Traci shares daily agendas and models the writing process; clusters of desks where small groups work on laying out a page or designing an advertisement; and individual work spaces at the computers. The materials necessary to initiate such activities are kept in a bookcase, readily accessible to students.

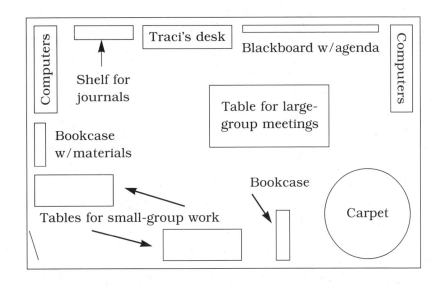

Learning to Do Projects: One Teacher's Success Story

All too often, we expect everything to go right the first time. Many curriculum packages reflect this expectation by offering a cookbook approach intended to minimize any problems that teachers might have. We too have tried to help you avoid or overcome many of the challenges related to a project-based approach to teaching. At the same time, however, we want to assure you that you *will* experience some difficulties you would not have if you had not invited your students to get up out of their seats and get genuinely involved in their own learning. Rather than prescribing a step-by-step lesson plan, we have encouraged you to design your own projects, try several out or try one project more than once, and give yourself time to learn how to deal with the challenges unique to projects. Anh's experience during her first year with projects provides an important case in point.

Like many teachers new to projects, Anh couldn't decide on a goal for her first project. She was unsure about what a "good" project goal was. She eventually chose to do a project in which the students were to decide how to use their playground time and space. She settled on this project because she had heard that students had complained about a lack of recess activities, and she thought they would be interested in solving the problem themselves. Her reasoning made the Playground Project a good one in terms of genuineness to the students, but it was not a topic or goal in which she was particularly interested. This would become a problem when the project became more demanding than she anticipated.

Not surprisingly, since this was her first try at a project, Anh was unclear about exactly how students would improve the playground. Were the students supposed to find a new area to play? To come up with new games? Or something else? As a result, the students did not have a clear understanding of what the possibilities were (putting in a full-size basketball court was out of the question, but it was still a popular idea!). In the first few meetings, Anh spent a lot of time trying to explain the general purpose of the project, rather than engaging students in brainstorming concrete ideas and making plans.

The project lacked momentum and everyone was frustrated. Eventually, feedback from other adults in the program helped Anh to identify a feasible concrete goal with the students. They decided to paint hockey and hopscotch boundaries on the blacktop. They completed this project successfully, but it had taken a long time to get started, and the term was almost over. In the end, Anh was unable to take full advantage of natural opportunities for learning.

During the second term, Anh's growing expertise was already evident. She didn't abandon everything she had tried the first term, but she picked a concrete and specific goal that was genuinely of interest to her: she asked the students to create their own board games. She brought in a game that she had created to show them and modeled how she came up with the idea. This gave her students a clear example of what they were expected to produce and a sense of the work they would have to do to create it (make a board, get pieces, invent rules, and so on). The students loved it! They had a great time coming up with games about everything from math to Malcolm X, and they celebrated at the end of the term with a party at which they invited their classmates to play their new games.

The project continued to improve the next time around. Anh's experiences allowed her to explain the goals of her project clearly and concisely, so that she didn't have to spend a long time lecturing to a large group. In addition to her own game, Anh was able to share some of the games the previous group had made. Further, she could anticipate the problems students were likely to encounter and help them either avoid or overcome them. Coming up with simple rules, for example, had not been as easy as she had expected. She experimented with ways to make the processes involved in writing rules clearer to students. In the end, all of these factors helped to make the students more self-directed and made it possible for Anh to act as a coach and to focus on coming up with creative ways to present and pursue her learning goals.

EPILOGUE

We have focused so far on the challenges involved in doing projects. Now may be a good time to remind you that projects present opportunities as well as challenges.

Perhaps the greatest opportunity that projects present is the chance to engage students in genuine work, thereby motivating them to get involved in their own learning. Take, for instance, a former student of ours named Jésus. Jésus was in the afterschool program the year it began. In that first year we had not fully developed our project approach, and the students were not accustomed to working independently on learning activities after school. On this particular day Jésus's teacher had arranged for his group to see a videotape about circuses in preparation for a circus they were going to perform. Given a piece of paper to jot down any ideas that occurred to him as he watched, he responded indignantly, "What's this? We're not supposed to do any work in here!"

Jésus was not alone in feeling that the afterschool program was no place for anything that resembled schoolwork. We had not yet created a classroom environment in which students felt comfortable, or even excited, about doing meaningful work. Two years later, however, we had learned how to design projects that were genuine contexts for learning—projects that appealed to the students while teaching them—and our students understood what was expected of them. When three girls approached the director of the program and asked if they could have the money needed to go on a field trip, he said, "Maybe — write me a proposal and I'll consider it." The girls had never been asked to do this before. To the director's delight and astonishment, they turned around, walked back to their classroom, and wrote a letter explaining where they wanted to go, why they wanted to go there, and how much it would cost. Soon afterward, all of the children in their group, both boys and girls, took to writing proposals like it was the only sensible thing to do. It was this unplanned event that led us to incorporate proposal writing into several of our projects.

At least as important as the chance for meaningful, real-world work are the opportunities projects present for self-direction. In fact, genuine work and self-direction can be a potent combination, as a student named Jade once demonstrated.

Jade, a fourth grader, was asked to call a local recycling center to arrange for the pickup of paper and plastic collected during the Better World Environmental Project. She immediately ran into difficulty. The phone book was a complete mystery to her, as was the rotary phone, which she looked at like it was an alien being. Jade looked to Doug, a volunteer at the school. He helped her figure out how to use the phone book and the phone and coached her on what to say when she made contact.

They hadn't anticipated the recorded voice-mail system. It completely baffled poor Jade. She persisted, though, and finally got a real person on the line. Doug heard a woman say hello and saw Jade choke, forgetting what to say. "Tell her who you are and why you are calling," he reminded her. Quickly recovering, Jade asked the perplexed secretary, "Who are you, and why are you calling?"

Realizing her mistake, Jade was mortified and hung up. The genuineness of the task and her responsibility for carrying it out, however, compelled her to try again— after all, the plastic and papers *must* get to the recycling center and she was in charge of arranging it! She tried again, with great success. Not long after, Jade was teaching other students how to use the phone book and what to do when a machine answers the phone.

These are just a few of our favorite stories from our days at the Mather School. To us, these anecdotes serve as reminders of what makes projects rewarding. They highlight what is special about the culture of a project-based classroom, a culture in which children happily engage in meaningful work, where student strengths are emphasized, where mistakes are recast as opportunities to learn, and where independence, reflection, and cooperation are valued and reinforced.

Best of luck with your efforts at creating a supportive and effective culture of learning through projects. We would love to hear from you about your experiences. We can be contacted at the Harvard Graduate School of Education, Longfellow Hall, Project Zero, Cambridge, MA 02138.

Assorted Questions and Answers

These are questions we are often asked about our work at
the Mather school:

Q: *How did you select students for the afterschool program?*

A: We experimented with a couple of approaches to student
selection, from selecting the most at-risk students in the
school to having interested students fill out applications
and admitting those whom the teachers and a guidance
counselor felt would benefit most. We recommend the
latter method because it helps ensure that participating students are interested in attending the program while at the
same time attending to the needs of the students.

Q: *What was your daily schedule?*

A: The program began at 3:00, Monday through Thursday.
Students met in the cafeteria, had a snack, and went outside or into the computer lab for free time until 3:30. Then
they broke up into their groups and went with their teachers to individual classrooms, where they worked on the projects until clean-up time—about 4:35. The bus arrived to
pick everyone up at 4:45. Although we managed to get a lot
done in this amount of time, we often felt that more time
would have been even better.

Q: *Did you mix third-, fourth-, and fifth-grade students within each group?*

A: Yes. Mixing age and ability groups worked well for us, partly because students helped and learned from each other. This cooperation freed the teachers to coach and to work with those students who needed them the most.

Q: *What was your student-to-teacher ratio?*

A: We had a ratio of one teacher to fifteen students, which is lower than many classrooms but higher than many afterschool programs. This should not be taken to mean that projects are inappropriate for larger classes, however. We have worked with many teachers who do projects with classes of twenty-five or more students during the regular school day.

Q: *What facilities did you have for the Cooking Project?*

A: None! We made do without a kitchen, a stove, or even a sink in the room. This forced us to find or create recipes that didn't require more than a hotplate or a blender. We managed quite well—see Appendix B for a list of recipes.

Q: *Where did you get the materials for your projects?*

A: We didn't have a lot of money for materials so, again, we made do. Except for the Etching Arts Project, none of the projects required unusual or expensive materials. We found we could scrounge in school closets, a local recycling center for teachers, and stationery and hardware stores for everything we needed.

Q: *What does it look like when a project is going well?*

A: We have asked that question ourselves. This is what a teacher from the Mather ASP told us:

I see lots of group work, a lot of hands-on type of things; I see the kids really working together, questioning each other about what they're doing, and it wouldn't be a quiet, "Sh, hush hush, sit down" type of situation. . . . [Students are] learning from each other, they're sharing their ideas, they are in discussion, and the teacher's going around questioning what they're writing.

—*Dominique*

Simple Recipes Used in the Cooking Project

Fruit Salad

1 orange   1 bunch seedless grapes

1 apple   1 banana

Peel orange and separate into sections. Peel and core the apple. Slice the apple. Remove all stems from grapes. Wash and drain grapes. Peel and slice banana. Mix fruit together.

Serves 3 or 4

Tuna Salad

1 can tuna   salt and pepper

1 tablespoon vinegar   lettuce, bread, or crackers

1/4 cup mayonnaise or plain yogurt

Other possible additions:

1 medium onion, 2 stalks celery, raisins, grapes, peanuts, or chopped pickles

Mix together the tuna, mayonnaise or yogurt, and vinegar. Add salt and pepper to taste and any other ingredients you want! Serve with lettuce, bread, or crackers.

Serves 4 or 5

No-Bake Cookies

2 cups sugar   1/3 cup shortening

1/2 cup milk

Mix together in pan. Heat and stir until mixture boils. Remove from heat. Add to milk mixture:

3 cups quick-cooking oatmeal   1/4 cup cocoa

1/2 cup peanut butter   1/2 teaspoon vanilla

Mix thoroughly. Drop by spoonfuls onto wax paper and cool.

Makes 3 dozen cookies

Coleslaw

1 head cabbage   3 tablespoons vinegar

3/4 cup mayonnaise   1/4 teaspoon salt

1/2 cup sour cream   pepper

Chop cabbage. Mix together mayonnaise, sour cream, and vinegar. Add cabbage to mayonnaise mixture. Add salt and pepper.

Makes about 6 cups coleslaw

Orange-Banana Shake

2 cups orange juice   1 ripe banana

Blend together in blender.

Serves 2

Angel Cookies

1/4 pound butter

3/4 cup sugar

1 cup crispy rice cereal

1 teaspoon vanilla

1/2 cup coconut

Mix butter and sugar together very well. In saucepan, simmer butter and sugar for about 3 minutes. Add vanilla and crispy rice cereal. Cool and form into small balls. Roll in coconut. No baking!

Makes 2 dozen cookies

Guacamole

2 large avocados

1 medium onion

2 ripe tomatoes

1/2 teaspoon vinegar or lemon juice

tortilla chips

Cut avocados in half and pry out pits. Scoop out avocado meat and mash in a bowl with a fork. Peel and chop onion and add to bowl. Cut tomatoes in small pieces and add to mashed avocado and chopped onion. Measure in vinegar or lemon juice and salt. Stir well. Serve with chips. Offer sour cream and salsa as well for a real treat!

Serves 4–6

Lemonade

4 lemons

1/2 cup sugar

3 1/2 cups water

Squeeze the lemons. Stir in sugar gradually. Add water.

Serves 6

Teaching Through Projects

Corn Salad

1 fourteen-ounce can whole-kernel corn   1 red bell pepper

1 small bunch green onions   10 cherry tomatoes

1 green bell pepper

Drain corn and put in large bowl. Chop green onions. Remove all seeds from peppers and chop them into small pieces. Cut tomatoes in half. Mix onions, peppers, and tomatoes with corn.

For dressing:

7 tablespoons olive oil   1/4 teaspoon mustard

2 tablespoons vinegar   salt and pepper

Mix mustard and vinegar. Slowly add olive oil. Add salt and pepper. Pour over cut-up vegetables and mix.

Serves 4

Grapes in Brown-Sugar Cream

1 1/2 lbs. seedless grapes   1 cup (1/2 pint) sour cream

1/2 cup brown sugar

Remove all stems from grapes. Rinse grapes in cold water. Drain. Dry on paper towels. In large bowl, mix brown sugar and sour cream. Blend well. Add grapes to bowl. Stir gently to coat all grapes. Refrigerate. Serve cold.

Serves 6

Onion Dip

1 pint sour cream

1 package onion-soup mix

potato chips or crackers

Mix together sour cream and onion-soup mix. Serve with crackers or chips.

Serves 6

Curry Dip

2 cups mayonnaise

juice of 1/2 lemon

2 tablespoons curry powder

tortilla or potato chips

raw vegetables (such as celery or carrot sticks)

Combine all ingredients. Refrigerate. Best if refrigerated for at least one day. Serve with vegetables and/or chips.

Serves 10

Mini Pizzas

1 package of 6 English muffins

1 cup shredded cheese of choice (such as mozzarella, jack, Cheddar)

1 cup tomato sauce

Cut the muffins in half. Pour some of the sauce on each muffin. Put some cheese on top. Bake in a toaster oven until the cheese begins to melt.

Makes 12 mini pizzas

Teaching Through Projects